LEARN HINDI IN 100 DAYS

THE 100% NATURAL METHOD TO FINALLY GET RESULTS WITH HINDI!

BEGINNER

NATURA LINGUA

NATURA
LINGUA

LEARN HINDI IN 100 DAYS

TABLE OF CONTENTS

Welcome xiii
The NaturaLingua Method xvii
Additional Resources xxi

BEFORE BEGINNING
Debunking Myths About Learning Hindi 3
Why learning Hindi? 6
The Polyglots' Secret 9

INSTRUCTIONS
Introduction to Devanagari Script 15
Hindi Pronunciation Guide for English Speakers 22
How to Use This Manual 27
And what about grammar? 33
Additional Resources 37

HINDI IN 100 DAYS
Important Notes 43
दिन 1: अभिवादन 44
Day 1: Greetings 45
दिन 2: आम वाक्यांश 46
Day 2: Common Expressions 47
दिन 3: परिचय संबंधी शब्दावली 48
Day 3: Introduction Vocabulary 49
दिन 4: व्यक्तिगत जानकारी 50
Day 4: Personal Information 51
दिन 5: सामान्य क्रियाएँ I 52
Day 5: Common Verbs I 53
दिन 6: पेय 54
Day 6: Beverages 55
Important Reminder Before Starting Lesson 7 56
57
दिन संख्या ७: वर्णनात्मक विशेषण I 58

Day 7: Descriptive Adjectives I 59
दिन 8: स्थान और दिशाएँ I 60
Day 8: Location and Directions I 61
दिन 9: स्थान और दिशाएँ Ii 62
Day 9: Location and Directions II 63
दिन 10: प्रश्न 64
Day 10: Questions 65
Challenge No. 1 # 66
67
दिन 11: दिन और समय 68
Day 11: Days and Time 69
दिन 12: सप्ताह के दिन 70
Day 12: Days of the Week 71
दिन 13: परिवार I 72
Day 13: Family I 73
दिन 14: परिवार Ii 74
Day 14: Family II 75
दिन 15: 1 से 10 तक की संख्याएँ 76
Day 15: Numbers from 1 to 10 77
दिन संख्या 16: 11 से 20 तक की संख्याएँ 78
Day 16: Numbers from 11 to 20 79
दिन 17: शॉपिंग I 80
Day 17: Shopping I 81
दिन 18: शॉपिंग Ii 82
Day 18: Shopping II 83
दिन 19: परिवहन I 84
Day 19: Transport I 85
दिन 20: परिवहन Ii 86
Day 20: Transport II 87
Challenge No. 2 # 88
89
दिन 21: स्थान और स्थल I 90
Day 21: Location and Places I 91
दिन 22: विशेषण Ii 92
Day 22: Adjectives II 93
दिन 23: विशेषण Iii 94
Day 23: Adjectives III 95
दिन 24: रंग 96
Day 24: Colors 97

दिन 25: इलेक्ट्रॉनिक्स और प्रौद्योगिकी I 98
Day 25: Electronics and Technology I 99
दिन 26: महीने और मौसम 100
Day 26: Months and Seasons 101
दिन 27: महीनों और मौसमों से परे 102
Day 27: Beyond months and seasons 103
दिन 28: भावनाएँ I 104
Day 28: Feelings I 105
दिन 29: भावनाएँ Ii 106
Day 29: Feelings II 107
दिन 30: शरीर के अंग I 108
Day 30: Body Parts I 109
Challenge No. 3 # 110
111
दिन 31: शरीर के अंग Ii 112
Day 31: Body Parts II 113
दिन 32: समय और कैलेंडर 114
Day 32: Time and Calendar 115
दिन 32: समय और कैलेंडर 116
Day 32: Time and Calendar 117
दिन 33: भोजन I 118
Day 33: Food I 119
दिन 34: खाद्य पदार्थ Ii 120
Day 34: Foods II 121
दिन 35: पेय पदार्थ और मिठाइयाँ 122
Day 35: Drinks and Desserts 123
दिन 36: खाना पकाने और रसोई 124
Day 36: Cooking and Kitchen 125
दिन 37: यात्रा और स्थान Ii 126
Day 37: Travel and Places II 127
दिन 38: आपातकाल और स्वास्थ्य 128
Day 38: Emergencies and Health 129
दिन 39: संख्याएँ 21-30 130
Day 39: Numbers 21-30 131
दिन 40: सप्ताह के दिन 132
Day 40: Days of the Week 133
Challenge No. 4 # 134
135
दिन 41: सफाई I 136

Day 41: Cleaning I 137
दिन 42: सफाई Ii 138
Day 42: Cleaning II 139
दिन 43: दिशा और स्थान Ii 140
Day 43: Direction and Location II 141
दिन 44: शॉपिंग Iii 142
Day 44: Shopping III 143
दिन 45: पैसे और भुगतान 144
Day 45: Money and Payments 145
दिन 46: समय और प्रकृति 146
Day 46: Weather and Nature 147
दिन 47: आपदाएँ और भूगोल 148
Day 47: Disasters and Geography 149
दिन 48: रंग 150
Day 48: Colors 151
दिन 49: प्रौद्योगिकी I 152
Day 49: Technology I 153
दिन 50: प्रौद्योगिकी Ii 154
Day 50: Technology II 155
Challenge No. 5 # 156
157
दिन 51: जानवर 158
Day 51: Animals 159
दिन 52: पौधे और प्रकृति 160
Day 52: Plants and Nature 161
दिन 53: संख्याएँ 31-40 162
Day 53: Numbers 31-40 163
दिन 54: संगीत और मनोरंजन 164
Day 54: Music and Entertainment 165
दिन 55: यात्रा और परिवहन Iii 166
Day 55: Travel and Transportation III 167
दिन 56: शॉपिंग Ii 168
Day 56: Shopping II 169
दिन 57: शरीर और स्वास्थ्य Ii 170
Day 57: Body and Health II 171
दिन 58: व्यवसाय और काम I 172
Day 58: Professions and Work I 173
दिन 59: घरेलू सामान Ii 174
Day 59: Household Items II 175

दिन 60: माप और आकार 176
Day 60: Measurements and Size 177
Challenge No. 6 # 178
179
दिन 61: भोजन और पोषण Ii 180
Day 61: Food and Nutrition II 181
दिन 62: सप्ताह के दिन 182
Day 62: Days of the Week 183
दिन 63: मौसम और ऋतुएँ 184
Day 63: Weather and Seasons 185
दिन 64: परिवार Ii 186
Day 64: Family II 187
दिन 65: दिशाएँ और स्थान Iii 188
Day 65: Directions and Locations III 189
दिन 66: भावनाएँ Ii 190
Day 66: Emotions II 191
दिन 67: प्रौद्योगिकी और मीडिया 192
Day 67: Technology and Media 193
दिन 68: पढ़ाई और कला 194
Day 68: Reading and Arts 195
दिन 69: यात्रा और स्थान Ii 196
Day 69: Travel and Places II 197
दिन 70: संख्याएँ 11-20 198
Day 70: Numbers 11-20 199
Challenge No. 7 # 200
201
दिन 71: 21 से 30 तक की संख्याएँ 202
Day 71: Numbers from 21 to 30 203
दिन 72: विविध I 204
Day 72: Miscellaneous I 205
दिन 73: रसोई और खाना पकाने Ii 206
Day 73: Cooking and Kitchen II 207
दिन 74: चिकित्सा और स्वास्थ्य Ii 208
Day 74: Medical and Health II 209
दिन 75: शिक्षा और सीखना 210
Day 75: Education and Learning 211
दिन 76: पैसा और शॉपिंग Ii 212
Day 76: Money and Shopping II 213
दिन 77: बाहर खाना Ii 214

Day 77: Eating Out II 215
दिन 78: घर और फर्नीचर Ii 216
Day 78: House and Furniture II 217
दिन 79: मौसम Ii 218
Day 79: Weather II 219
दिन 80: शौक और हॉबीज Ii 220
Day 80: Leisure and Hobbies II 221
Challenge No. 8 # 222
223
दिन 81: परिवहन Ii 224
Day 81: Transport II 225
दिन 82: प्रकृति और भूगोल Ii 226
Day 82: Nature and Geography II 227
दिन 83: समय और दिनचर्या 228
Day 83: Time and Routine 229
दिन 84: भावनाएँ Iii 230
Day 84: Emotions III 231
दिन 85: रंग और आकार 232
Day 85: Colors and Shapes 233
दिन 86: संबंध 234
Day 86: Relationships 235
दिन 87: कपड़े और सामान 236
Day 87: Clothes and Accessories 237
दिन 88: प्रौद्योगिकी और मीडिया Ii 238
Day 88: Technology and Media II 239
दिन 89: खाना और पेय Ii 240
Day 89: Food and Drinks II 241
दिन 90: घर और जीवन 242
Day 90: Home and Life 243
Challenge No. 9 # 244
245
दिन 91: शॉपिंग और दुकानें 246
Day 91: Shopping and Stores 247
दिन 92: आपातकाल और सुरक्षा 248
Day 92: Emergency and Safety 249
दिन 93: यात्रा और स्थान Iii 250
Day 93: Travel and Places III 251
दिन 94: जानवर और पालतू जानवर 252
Day 94: Animals and Pets 253

दिन 95: काम और पेशा 254
Day 95: Work and Profession 255
दिन 96: दिन और महीने 256
Day 96: Days and Months 257
दिन 97: शरीर और स्वास्थ्य 258
Day 97: Body and Health 259
दिन 98: शिक्षा और सीखने का दूसरा भाग 260
Day 98: Education and Learning II 261
दिन 99: विविध Ii 262
Day 99: Miscellaneous II 263
दिन 100: मैनुअल पूरा करने के लिए बधाई हो 264
Day 100: Congratulations on completing the manual 265
Challenge No. 10 # 266
267

CONGRATULATIONS AND NEXT STEPS
Congratulations 271
What's Next? 273
Additional Resources 275
About the Author 277
Share Your Experience 278
By the Same Author 279

Essential Glossary 281

WELCOME

Imagine: you're walking around in Delhi, understanding and speaking Hindi naturally. Phrases spontaneously emerge in your mind, and you navigate this new language with ease and fluidity.

That's the goal of this manual.

If you're reading these lines, it's because you wish to master Hindi. Whether for work or pleasure, the goal remains the same: to achieve it. The problem lies in the lack of time. Good courses to learn Hindi in English are rare, and often, the available methods are complicated or ineffective.

But your motivation is intact! That's why you've tried apps promising wonders in just a few minutes a day. The result? More time spent collecting badges than acquiring real skills in Hindi. You've tried traditional textbooks, often too complex and focused on grammar. Perhaps you've even considered classical courses, incompatible with your schedule.

My name is François, and I'm French. I am well acquainted with this situation.

A few years ago, I went to do a year of volunteering in Ukraine. To be effective, I had to quickly learn Russian and English. But most learning resources were either too superficial or too complex.

Even worse, despite my motivation and long hours in front of my screen or immersed in manuals, the results were not forthcoming. I felt frustrated, angry, wondering why language learning seemed so easy for some and so difficult for me.

I was about to give up, thinking I was not cut out for languages.

Then, one evening, I met an English polyglot who spoke 11 languages. Impressed by his linguistic abilities, I asked him for his secret. His answer, as simple as it was unexpected, was that one should not study a language, but live it! One must learn a new language as one learned their mother tongue.

Intrigued, I followed his advice.

After all, I hadn't learned my mother tongue through conjugation tables or collecting badges. No, I learned French by imitating those around me, by communicating with my friends and family.

So, I abandoned my textbooks and removed the conjugation tables from the walls of my room.

I started listening to podcasts in English, watching movies in Russian, and engaging in my first conversations. Forgetting grammar and conjugation, I simply used these languages. The results were quick to come: I increasingly understood daily conversations, with words and phrases naturally coming to mind.

My English friend was right: it worked.

Just as it's more effective to learn to swim by jumping into the water rather than reading a book on swimming, learning a foreign language is done by immersing oneself in the language, practicing conversation, listening, and adapting to the culture and linguistic nuances, rather than limiting oneself to the theoretical study of grammar rules and vocabulary.

This is the approach I propose in this Natura Lingua manual.

From the first lesson, you will fully immerse yourself in Hindi.

In a few days, or even weeks, you will start to build a lexical foundation and mental mechanisms that will allow you to understand and communicate naturally in most daily situations.

Be aware, Natura Lingua is not a miracle solution. To get results, you will need to follow one lesson a day for 100 days.

But if you're ready to make this effort, then anyone can succeed with our method, based directly on the mechanisms that allowed you to learn your mother tongue.

If you've already learned your mother tongue, why couldn't you learn Hindi?

Shabash (शाबाश),

François

THE NATURALINGUA METHOD

Natura Lingua offers you a natural and intuitive approach that transforms the language learning experience. Every educational content is meticulously optimized to enable you to acquire a new language up to 10 times faster and more efficiently than traditional methods.

Each Natura Lingua manual is based on four innovative principles that reinvent the way languages are learned.

1. The Funnel Principle

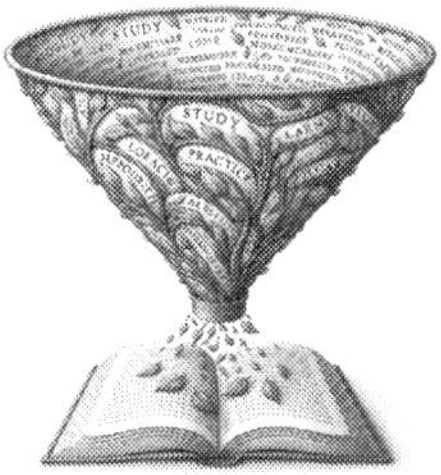

We've rigorously analyzed and filtered hundreds of thousands of words to retain only those that are essential in daily conversations. Thanks to this principle, you quickly develop a high level of understanding without wasting your time on superfluous terms.

2. Contextual Assimilation

Each term is introduced in a natural setting, reflecting common daily interactions. The result? A smooth assimilation of hundreds of terms and expressions, without ever feeling like you're actually studying.

3. Progressive Overload

Each lesson meticulously presents new words while reintroducing those already studied. Thus, day by day, you continuously progress while consolidating what you've learned.

4. Multiple Integrated Revisions

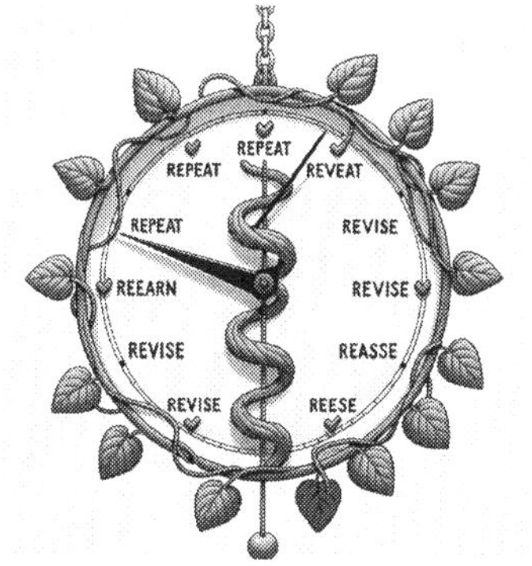

Gone are the days when vocabulary seemed to evaporate from your memory. Our unique method ensures that each term is reintroduced at strategic intervals in subsequent lessons. You revisit each term up to four times, reinforcing its memorization without even realizing it.

The Mechanism

What makes "Natura Lingua" so effective is its natural and gradual learning. Each lesson introduces new words in bold while reusing words from previous lessons. Additionally, each lesson is enriched with a "Grammatical Note" to illuminate key aspects of the language and a "Cultural Note" to avoid faux pas during conversations with natives.

Is It For Me?

If you're looking to speak a new language without getting lost in the intricacies of grammar, this manual is for you. However, if you love complex grammatical rules and endless vocabulary lists, then this manual is not for you.

Integrating the Manual Into Your Daily Life

Create a routine: dedicate a slot each day for your 15-minute lesson. A coffee in hand, your manual open in front of you, and off you go!

NB. I highly recommend downloading the audio that accompanies the lessons. It will greatly enhance your understanding and pronunciation. Using this manual without the audio is like enjoying toast without jam: you're missing the essence.

ADDITIONAL RESOURCES

DOWNLOAD THE RESOURCES ASSOCIATED WITH THIS MANUAL AND GREATLY ENHANCE YOUR CHANCES OF SUCCESS.

Scan this QR code to access them:

SCAN ME

https://www.natura-lingua.com/download

- **Optimize your learning with audio:** To significantly improve your language skills, we strongly advise you to download the audio files accompanying this manual. This will enhance your listening comprehension and pronunciation.

- **Enhance your learning with flashcards:** Flashcards are excellent tools for vocabulary memorization. We highly encourage you to use them to maximize your results. Download our set of cards, specially designed for this manual.
- **Join our learning community:** If you're looking to connect with other language enthusiasts through "Natura Lingua", we invite you to join our online group. In this community, you'll have the opportunity to ask questions, find learning partners, and share your progress.
- **Explore more with other Natura Lingua manuals:** If you like this method, note that there are other similar manuals for different languages. Discover our complete collection of manuals to enrich your linguistic learning experience in a natural and progressive way.

We are here to support you in learning the target language. For optimal results, we highly recommend downloading the audio and using the flashcards. These additional resources are designed to further facilitate your journey.

Happy learning!

BEFORE BEGINNING

DEBUNKING MYTHS ABOUT LEARNING HINDI

One of the most pervasive myths about learning Hindi is that it is an exceptionally difficult language to master, especially for English speakers. This belief can be daunting for potential learners, creating an invisible barrier that prevents many from even attempting to learn this beautiful and culturally rich language. However, the reality is far more encouraging and nuanced than this initial apprehension suggests. Let's explore and debunk some common myths about learning Hindi, shedding light on the true nature of this linguistic journey.

Myth 1: Hindi is Too Difficult for English Speakers

The idea that Hindi is inherently more difficult than other languages is a misconception. While Hindi does have a different script (Devanagari) and grammatical structure, it is by no means an insurmountable challenge. Many English words are borrowed from Hindi, such as 'yoga', 'jungle', and 'karma', making some vocabulary surprisingly familiar.

Moreover, the phonetic nature of the Devanagari script actually makes pronunciation clearer once the basics are mastered.

Myth 2: You Need to Be Young to Learn Hindi

Another common myth is that language learning is only for the young. However, studies have shown that adults are capable of learning new languages to fluency. What matters more is motivation, consistent practice, and a positive mindset. Adults often have better metacognitive skills and learning strategies than children, which can be a significant advantage.

Myth 3: You Must Travel to India to Learn Hindi Properly

While immersion is a powerful tool in language learning, it's not the only path to fluency. With the advent of the internet, resources for learning Hindi have become more accessible than ever. Online courses, language exchange partners, and multimedia resources can provide a comprehensive learning experience from anywhere in the world.

Myth 4: Hindi Isn't Useful Outside of India

Hindi is the fourth most spoken language in the world, with a vast diaspora. Learning Hindi opens up not just India but communities worldwide, including in Nepal, Mauritius, Fiji, Suriname, Guyana, Trinidad & Tobago, and South Africa. Moreover, understanding Hindi allows for a deeper appreciation of Bollywood films, Indian literature, and philosophies without the barrier of translation.

Myth 5: It Takes Years to Achieve Basic Communication

Many learners find that they can start having basic conversations within a few months of dedicated study. The key is focusing on practical vocabulary and phrases used in daily life. Success stories abound of learners who achieved conversational fluency within a year, using their skills to enhance travels, form new friendships, and even advance their careers.

The true challenge in learning Hindi—or any language—is not inherent difficulty but maintaining consistency and motivation. Language learning is a marathon, not a sprint. Setting realistic goals, celebrating small victories, and integrating Hindi into your daily life through music, films, and conversation can make the journey enjoyable and rewarding.

The myths surrounding the learning of Hindi often overshadow the reality: with the right approach, learning Hindi is an attainable and profoundly enriching goal. By debunking these myths, we hope to encourage more language enthusiasts to embark on the journey of learning Hindi, discovering not just a new way of communicating, but a new way of seeing the world.

WHY LEARNING HINDI?

If you're reading this text, it's because you're interested in learning Hindi. That's a fantastic choice! Hindi, a language that bridges continents and cultures, is not just a means of communication but a gateway to a rich historical and cultural heritage.

Let's talk about motivation. Learning a new language, especially one as dynamic and beautiful as Hindi, can be a journey filled with excitement, challenges, and unparalleled satisfaction. But what keeps us going when the going gets tough? What fuels our desire to push through the difficult phases of language learning?

Here are 7 sources of inspiration/motivation/reason to stimulate the learner's desire to learn Hindi, each presented in a way to reignite your passion and commitment:

. . .

1. **Cultural Immersion:** Learning Hindi opens up the vast and diverse world of Indian culture. From Bollywood movies and music to literature and festivals, your understanding and appreciation of these cultural phenomena will deepen immeasurably.

2. **Career Opportunities:** In an increasingly globalized world, proficiency in Hindi offers a competitive edge in fields such as international relations, business, and technology, where India plays a key role.

3. **Personal Connections:** Hindi allows you to connect on a deeper level with Hindi-speaking friends, family, or anyone you meet on your travels. It's about building bridges and forming lasting relationships.

4. **Travel:** India is a land of incredible diversity and beauty. Knowing Hindi enriches your travel experiences, allowing you to explore off-the-beaten-path destinations and interact with locals in a more meaningful way.

5. **Intellectual Challenge:** Learning a new language is a fantastic way to stimulate your brain, improve cognitive skills, and even delay the onset of dementia. Hindi, with its unique script and grammar, offers a rewarding challenge.

. . .

6. **Spiritual Exploration:** For those interested in yoga, meditation, or spirituality, learning Hindi can deepen your understanding and appreciation of these practices, many of which are rooted in ancient Indian texts.

7. **Personal Growth:** The process of learning Hindi is a journey of self-discovery. It challenges your limits, expands your worldview, and teaches you the value of perseverance and hard work.

Let this be a call to action for all aspiring Hindi learners. Embrace the challenges, celebrate the victories, and never lose sight of why you started this journey. The road to mastering Hindi may be long, but it is filled with moments of joy, discovery, and profound personal growth. Keep pushing forward, keep practicing, and most importantly, keep enjoying every step of your learning journey. Your dedication to learning Hindi will not only enrich your life but also open doors to a world you might never have imagined.

THE POLYGLOTS' SECRET

Have you ever thought that learning multiple languages was only for geniuses? Take Cardinal Giuseppe Mezzofanti, for example—he's said to have spoken between 38 and 72 languages, depending on the source. And what makes it even more impressive is that he did it in a time without the internet, apps, or all the resources we have today. Another amazing example is Kato Lomb, a Hungarian interpreter who spoke 16 languages fluently and could handle 11 more.

But how did they do it?

These language masters understood something many people miss. Learning a language doesn't have to mean complicated textbooks, intense courses, or years of effort. Mezzofanti and Lomb used a simpler, more natural approach. For them, learning wasn't a chore or an impossible task—it was a smooth, almost instinctive process.

. . .

What if learning a language wasn't as hard as you think?

A lot of people believe that becoming a polyglot takes a special gift or years of hard work. But that's not true. Learning a language is often much easier than it seems. What feels like a huge challenge is really just about using the right method.

Mezzofanti learned by translating religious texts, while Kato Lomb translated foreign books she found in libraries. This helped them learn quickly and naturally. Their secret? Consistency and immersion through translation. By translating texts from a foreign language into their own, and then back again, they slowly mastered the language.

So how can you do the same?

You don't need expensive courses or complicated techniques. Start with simple texts in the language you want to learn, translate them into your own language, and then back again. This simple method helps you absorb the language and its structure naturally.

Now's the time to get started.

With the NaturaLingua method, inspired by the natural approaches of Mezzofanti and Lomb, you can finally break through the language barrier. Don't let fear or misconceptions stop you. Jump in and enjoy the process of learning, understanding, and speaking a new language, one translation at a time. Are you ready to take on the challenge and add new languages to your life?

INSTRUCTIONS

INTRODUCTION TO DEVANAGARI SCRIPT

The Devanagari script is used for several languages, including Hindi, Marathi, and Sanskrit. Unlike the Latin alphabet, Devanagari is an abugida, meaning each character represents a consonant with an inherent vowel sound, which can be changed with the use of diacritical marks.

Understanding the Basics

- **Consonants**: Devanagari consists of 33 basic consonants. Each consonant has an inherent 'a' sound. For example, the letter क is pronounced 'ka'. To modify the inherent vowel, diacritics are used.
- **Vowels**: There are 12 basic vowel sounds in Devanagari. These can be written as independent letters when they occur at the beginning of a word or as diacritical marks when they modify a consonant.

- **Vowel Diacritics**: Vowel diacritics are marks that attach to consonants to change their inherent 'a' sound to another vowel. For instance, the diacritic for 'i' is ी, changing क (ka) to की (ki).
- **Consonant Clusters (Jodakshar)**: When two or more consonants come together in a word without intervening vowels, they form a consonant cluster. These are represented by combining the constituent consonants into a single glyph or by using a special symbol called a "virama" to denote the absence of an inherent vowel.
- **The Schwa Syncope Rule**: In Hindi, the inherent 'a' sound of a consonant is often not pronounced at the end of a word or in certain consonant clusters. This phenomenon is known as the "schwa syncope" and is an important aspect of pronunciation.

Learning to Read

- **Start with Vowels**: Familiarize yourself with the 12 vowel sounds and their independent forms. Practice writing and pronouncing them.
- **Move to Consonants**: Learn the 33 consonants, paying attention to their inherent 'a' sound. Practice writing and pronouncing simple consonant-vowel combinations.
- **Practice with Diacritics**: Learn the vowel diacritics and practice modifying consonant

sounds with them. This will help you read and write more complex words.

- **Consonant Clusters**: Start recognizing and practicing consonant clusters. Use resources like textbooks or language learning apps for guided practice.

Vowels and Their Independent Forms

In Hindi, vowels can appear at the beginning of a word or syllable and have independent forms. There are 12 primary vowels in Hindi:

1. अ (a)
2. आ (ā)
3. इ (i)
4. ई (ī)
5. उ (u)
6. ऊ (ū)
7. ए (e)
8. ऐ (ai)
9. ओ (o)
10. औ (au)
11. ऋ (ṛ)
12. ॠ (ṝ)

These vowels can stand alone or modify consonants when attached as diacritical marks.

. . .

Consonants

Hindi consonants are categorized based on their place and mode of articulation. There are 33 primary consonants:

1. **Velar Consonants** : Produced with the back of the tongue against the soft palate.

- क (ka)
- ख (kha)
- ग (ga)
- घ (gha)
- ङ (ṅa)

2. **Palatal Consonants**: Produced with the body of the tongue raised against the hard palate.

- च (ca)
- छ (cha)
- ज (ja)
- झ (jha)
- ञ (ña)

3. **Retroflex Consonants**: Produced by curling the tongue back against the roof of the mouth.

- ट (ṭa)
- ठ (ṭha)
- ड (ḍa)
- ढ (ḍha)
- ण (ṇa)

4. **Dental Consonants** : Produced with the tongue against the upper teeth.

- त (ta)
- थ (tha)
- द (da)
- ध (dha)
- न (na)

5. **Labial Consonants**: Produced with the lips.

- प (pa)
- फ (pha)
- ब (ba)
- भ (bha)
- म (ma)

6. **Semi-vowels/Yamātārajabhānasalagam**: Representing approximant sounds and nasal sounds.

- य (ya)
- र (ra)
- ल (la)
- व (va)
- श (śa)
- ष (ṣa)
- स (sa)
- ह (ha)
- ळ (ḷa)

7. **Additional Consonants**: Used in Sanskrit and other

languages.

- क्ष (kṣa)
- त्र (tra)
- ज्ञ (jña)

Vowel Diacritics (Matras)

Vowel sounds in Hindi modify consonant sounds through the use of diacritic marks called matras. Each vowel has a corresponding matra that attaches to a consonant to change its inherent 'a' sound to that of the vowel. For example, the consonant क (ka) can be modified to कि (ki) using the diacritic for 'i'.

1. ा (ā) - Makes the vowel sound long (a → ā).
2. ि (i) - Adds an 'i' sound.
3. ी (ī) - Long 'i' sound.
4. ु (u) - Adds a 'u' sound.
5. ू (ū) - Long 'u' sound.
6. े (e) - Adds an 'e' sound.
7. ै (ai) - Adds an 'ai' sound.
8. ो (o) - Adds an 'o' sound.
9. ौ (au) - Adds an 'au' sound.
10. ृ (ṛ) - Adds a 'ṛ' sound.
11. ॄ (ṝ) - Long 'ṛ' sound.

Consonant Clusters and the Virama

When consonants occur together without a vowel sound in between, they form clusters known as conjuncts. A special character called the virama (्) is used to suppress the inherent 'a' sound of a consonant when it's part of a cluster.

For instance, to create a cluster with 'k' (क) and 't' (त), the virama is placed after 'k', and then 't' is added (क्त).

Understanding these components is fundamental to reading and writing in Hindi. Practice is essential, as familiarity with the script will make it easier to recognize patterns and common word formations.

HINDI PRONUNCIATION GUIDE FOR ENGLISH SPEAKERS

Welcome to your quick guide to Hindi pronunciation! Hindi sounds can be quite distinct from English, but with this guide, you'll get a basic understanding of how to approach them. Remember, practice is key!

Vowels

1. **अ a** as in America. Example: kamal (lotus)
2. **आ aa** as in father. Example: baat (talk)
3. **इ i** as in sit. Example: kitab (book)
4. **ई ee** as in see. Example: neend (sleep)
5. **उ u** as in put. Example: kursi (chair)
6. **ऊ oo** as in food. Example: julool (swing)
7. **ए e** as in cafe. Example: lekin (but)
8. **ऐ ai** as in ride. Example: bail (ox)
9. **ओ o** as in orange. Example: bol (speak)
10. **औ au** as in house. Example: gaum (village)

. . .

Consonants

1. **क k** as in kite. Example: kalam (pen)
2. **ख kh** as a strong, breathy k. Think of the Scottish loch. Example: khana (food)
3. **ग g** as in go. Example: gadi (vehicle)
4. **घ gh** as a more voiced version of kh. Example: ghar (home)
5. **च ch** as in chat. Example: chai (tea)
6. **छ chh** as a more aspirated ch. Example: chhota (small)
7. **ज j** as in jug. Example: jungle (forest)
8. **झ jh** as a more voiced version of chh. Example: jharoo (broom)
9. **ट t** as a retroflex, tongue curled back. Example: tota (parrot)
10. **ठ th** as a more aspirated t. Example: thanda (cold)
11. **ड d** as a retroflex, more intense d. Example: danda (stick)
12. **ढ dh** as a more aspirated d. Example: dhoop (sunshine)
13. **न n** as in no. Example: namak (salt)
14. **प p** as in pan. Example: patang (kite)
15. **फ ph** as a more aspirated p. Example: phool (flower)
16. **ब b** as in bat. Example: bandar (monkey)
17. **भ bh** as a more voiced version of ph. Example: bhaloo (bear)
18. **म m** as in man. Example: matka (pot)

19. **य y** as in yes. Example: yatra (journey)
20. **र r** as a rolled r. Example: rassi (rope)
21. **ल l** as in love. Example: lal (red)
22. **व v/w** as in van or water. Example: van (forest)
23. **श sh** as in ship. Example: shakkar (sugar)
24. **ष Sh** as a more retroflex sh. Example: shatkon (hexagon)
25. **स s** as in sun. Example: sabun (soap)
26. **ह h** as in hat. Example: hathi (elephant)

Special Sounds

1. **ऋ ri** as in the ri in riddle. Example: kriti (creation)
2. **ऐं aim** as in aim. Example: aimbar (sky)
3. **औं aum** as in home with a nasal sound. Example: aum (Om)

Nasal Sounds

Nasal sounds are often indicated by a dot (ँ) or a small 'n' (ं) above consonants. They add a nasal quality to the vowel sound of the syllable.

Tone and Stress

Hindi does not have a stress accent like English. The

rhythm of a Hindi sentence is more even, and all syllables are generally given equal emphasis.

Practice Makes Perfect

The best way to master Hindi pronunciation is to listen and practice regularly. Try repeating words, watching Hindi movies, or listening to Hindi music to get accustomed to the sounds.

Happy learning!

HOW TO USE THIS MANUAL

Phase No. 1:

1. Read the text in the language you are learning out loud, while listening to the corresponding audio (to be downloaded).
2. Try to translate the text into English, without consulting the translation.
3. Check with the official translation to complete yours.

This phase facilitates the assimilation of the language structure and vocabulary and reinforces understanding.

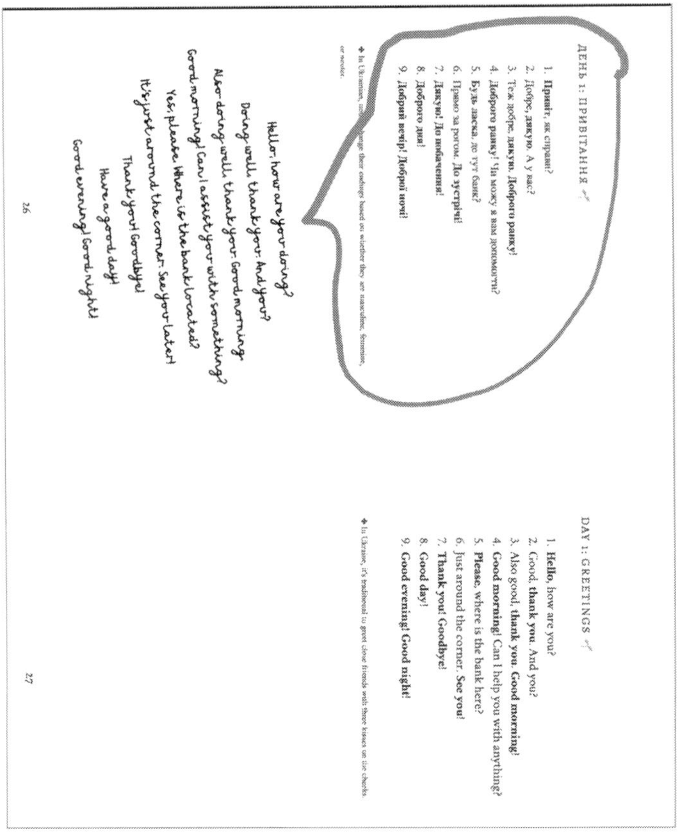
ДЕНЬ 1: ПРИВІТАННЯ
1. Привіт, як справи?
2. Добре, дякую. А у вас?
3. Теж добре, дякую. Доброго ранку!
4. Доброго ранку! Чи можу я вам допомогти?
5. Будь ласка, де тут банк?
6. Прямо за рогом. До зустрічі!
7. Дякую! До побачення!
8. Доброго дня!
9. Добрий вечір! Доброї ночі!
Hello, how are you doing?
Doing well, thank you. And you?
Also doing well, thank you. Good morning.
Good morning! Can I assist you with something?
Yes, please. Where is the bank located?
It's just around the corner. See you later!
Thank you! Goodbye!
Have a good day!
Good evening! Good night!
26
DAY 1: GREETINGS
1. Hello, how are you?
2. Good, thank you. And you?
3. Also good, thank you. Good morning!
4. Good morning! Can I help you with anything?
5. Please, where is the bank here?
6. Just around the corner. See you!
7. Thank you! Goodbye!
8. Good day!
9. Good evening! Good night!
In Ukraine, it's traditional to greet close friends with three kisses on the cheeks.
27

Phase No. 1

Phase No. 2 (starting from lesson No. 7):

1. For each lesson starting from No. 7, first translate the text of that lesson (No. 7, No. 8, etc.) from the target language into English.
2. Then, go back 6 lessons and translate the English version of that lesson's text from English back into the target language, without referring to the original text.
3. Compare your translation with the original text of that lesson and adjust if necessary.
4. Read aloud the original text of that lesson, while listening to the audio.

This phase stimulates the activation of already acquired vocabulary and promotes the improvement of your communication skills.

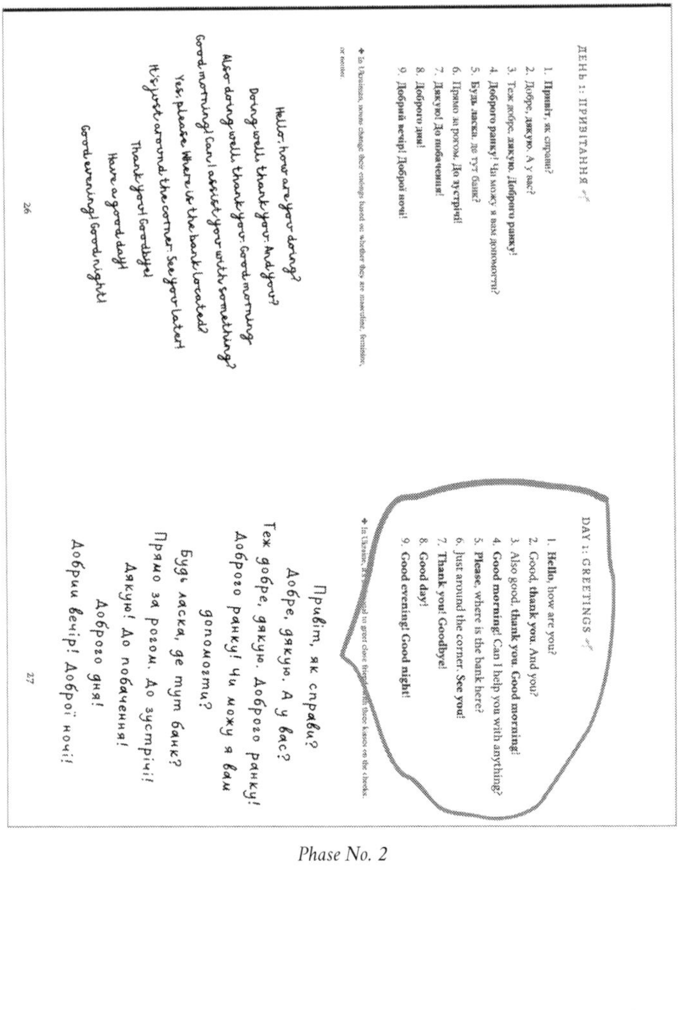

ДЕНЬ 1: ПРИВІТАННЯ

1. **Привіт**, як справи?
2. Добре, **дякую**. А у вас?
3. Теж добре, **дякую**. **Доброго ранку!**
4. **Доброго ранку!** Чи можу я вам допомогти?
5. **Будь ласка**, де тут банк?
6. Прямо за рогом. **До зустрічі!**
7. **Дякую! До побачення!**
8. **Доброго дня!**
9. **Добрий вечір! Доброї ночі!**

✦ In Ukrainian, nouns change their endings based on whether they are masculine, feminine, or neuter.

Hello, how are you doing?
Doing well, thank you. And you?
Also doing well, thank you. Good morning
Good morning! Can I assist you with something?
Yes, please. Where is the bank located?
It's just around the corner. See you later!
Thank you! Goodbye!
Have a good day!
Good evening! Good night!

26

DAY 1: GREETINGS

1. **Hello**, how are you?
2. Good, **thank you**. And you?
3. Also good, **thank you**. **Good morning!**
4. **Good morning!** Can I help you with anything?
5. **Please**, where is the bank here?
6. Just around the corner. **See you!**
7. **Thank you! Goodbye!**
8. **Good day!**
9. **Good evening! Good night!**

✦ In Ukraine, it's ... to greet close friends with three kisses on the cheeks.

Привіт, як справи?
Добре, дякую. А у вас?
Теж добре, дякую. Доброго ранку!
Доброго ранку! Чи можу я вам допомогти?
Будь ласка, де тут банк?
Прямо за рогом. До зустрічі!
Дякую! До побачення!
Доброго дня!
Добрии вечір! Доброї ночі!

27

Phase No. 2

Continue in the same way for the following lessons. For example, for lesson No. 8, first translate the text of lesson No. 8 from the target language into English, then translate the text of lesson No. 2 from English back into the target language, and so on.

Additionally, every 10 lessons, a small challenge awaits you to put your knowledge into practice.

Note: Your translations do not need to match the manual texts perfectly, but they should convey a similar meaning. If you are using the paper version of the manual, note your translations directly at the bottom of the text, or else use a separate notebook.

AND WHAT ABOUT GRAMMAR?

You've probably been told that mastering a language starts with grammar. But this traditional approach is not only discouraging, it's also counterproductive. Learning a language is really about diving into a living world and understanding how words and sentences come to life in real situations, not by endlessly reciting rules.

One of the biggest mistakes many learners make is trying to memorize grammar rules by heart. It's tedious, demotivating, and ineffective. Why? Because our brains remember things that make sense and are used regularly. Rules without context are quickly forgotten. It's disconnected from real-life learning: instead of speaking, feeling, and immersing yourself in the language, you end up drowning in sterile theories.

We strongly believe that grammar shouldn't be learned before using a language, but rather through natural usage.

Our method is based on a simple principle: start by using the language, then adjust your understanding of grammar as it comes up in real-life situations. You learn to speak and understand, just like a child discovering their native language. When a grammar question arises, you find the answer and remember it because it's relevant at that moment.

How does it work in practice?

1. Immerse yourself in the language without worrying about grammar rules at first.
2. When a grammar question naturally comes up ("Why is this word used here?"), look for the answer.
3. Write down the grammar points you come across on a separate page or in the blank section of this manual, like a grammar journal.
4. Keep repeating this process, question after question, and watch how your understanding grows without feeling like you're studying.

By using this method, you'll see real results: each grammar point is anchored in a real context, making it easier to remember and longer-lasting. Instead of getting stuck in grammar books, you'll be using the language right away, gaining confidence and fluency in your communication. Plus, you'll enjoy it more—learning becomes an exciting journey where each discovery is a personal victory.

Grammar will become an ally, not a hurdle, helping you progress naturally and smoothly.

With Natura Lingua, you're not following a rigid method—you're living the language. Grammar is no longer a mountain to climb, but a natural path that unfolds as you go, step by step.

ADDITIONAL RESOURCES

DOWNLOAD THE RESOURCES ASSOCIATED WITH THIS MANUAL AND GREATLY ENHANCE YOUR CHANCES OF SUCCESS.

Scan this QR code to access them:

SCAN ME

https://www.natura-lingua.com/download

• **Optimize your learning with audio:** To significantly improve your language skills, we strongly advise you to download the audio files accompanying this manual. This will enhance your listening comprehension and pronunciation.

• **Enhance your learning with flashcards:** Flashcards are excellent tools for vocabulary memorization. We highly encourage you to use them to maximize your results. Download our set of cards, specially designed for this manual.

• **Join our learning community:** If you're looking to connect with other language enthusiasts through "Natura Lingua", we invite you to join our online group. In this community, you'll have the opportunity to ask questions, find learning partners, and share your progress.

• **Explore more with other Natura Lingua manuals:** If you like this method, note that there are other similar manuals for different languages. Discover our complete collection of manuals to enrich your linguistic learning experience in a natural and progressive way.

We are here to support you in learning the target language. For optimal results, we highly recommend downloading the audio and using the flashcards. These additional resources are designed to further facilitate your journey.

Happy learning!

HINDI IN 100 DAYS

Check off a box below after completing each lesson. This will aid you in monitoring your progress and maintaining motivation throughout your learning experience.

☒ ☐ ☐ ☐ ☐ ☐ ☐ ☐ ☐ ☐
☐ ☐ ☐ ☐ ☐ ☐ ☐ ☐ ☐ ☐
☐ ☐ ☐ ☐ ☐ ☐ ☐ ☐ ☐ ☐
☐ ☐ ☐ ☐ ☐ ☐ ☐ ☐ ☐ ☐
☐ ☐ ☐ ☐ ☐ ☐ ☐ ☐ ☐ ☐
☐ ☐ ☐ ☐ ☐ ☐ ☐ ☐ ☐ ☐
☐ ☐ ☐ ☐ ☐ ☐ ☐ ☐ ☐ ☐
☐ ☐ ☐ ☐ ☐ ☐ ☐ ☐ ☐ ☐
☐ ☐ ☐ ☐ ☐ ☐ ☐ ☐ ☐ ☐
☐ ☐ ☐ ☐ ☐ ☐ ☐ ☐ ☐ ☐

IMPORTANT NOTES :

1. **The Essentials: Vocabulary and Key Phrases:** In each Natura Lingua lesson, we carefully select the most useful words and expressions relevant to the theme studied. The goal is to familiarize you with the most frequently used constructions in the target language. Sometimes, the general meaning of the texts might seem surprising, but don't worry, it's an essential part of our method. It helps you focus on the practical aspects of the language, thereby accelerating your learning for better understanding and more effective communication.

2. **Translation: As Close to the Original as Possible:** We translate in a way that stays true to the source text, capturing how sentences are structured and ideas are conveyed in the target language. Our goal is not syntactic perfection in English, but rather to give you an authentic insight into the thought process and structure of the language you are learning. This method immerses you in the language, allowing you to gain a more natural and intuitive understanding. Our aim is to help you think and communicate fluently in the learned language, not just understand it. We want to prepare you to use the language practically and confidently in your daily life.

दिन 1: अभिवादन

1. **नमस्ते**, आप कैसे हैं?
2. **नमस्ते**, मैं ठीक हूँ, धन्यवाद। और आप?
3. मैं भी ठीक हूँ। **शुभ संध्या**।
4. **शुभ संध्या**। आप सोने जा रहे हैं?
5. हाँ, मैं थक गया हूँ। **शुभ रात्रि**।
6. **शुभ रात्रि**। **फिर मिलेंगे**।
7. ज़रूर, **फिर मिलेंगे**। **अलविदा**।
8. **कोई बात नहीं**, **अलविदा**।

✣ In Hindi, nouns like "नमस्ते" (Namaste) for greeting change form based on number and gender.

1. **namaste**, āp kaise haiṁ?
2. **namaste**, maiṁ ṭhīk hūṁ, dhanyavād. aur āp?
3. maiṁ bhī ṭhīk hūṁ. **śubh sandhyā**.
4. **śubh sandhyā**. āp sone jā rahe haiṁ?
5. hāṁ, maiṁ thak gayā hūṁ. **śubh rātri**.
6. **śubh rātri**. **phir milenge**.
7. zarūr, **phir milenge**. **alavidā**.
8. **koī bāt nahīṁ**, **alavidā**.

1. **Hello**, how are you?
2. **Hello**, I'm fine, thank you. And you?
3. I'm also fine. **Good evening**.
4. **Good evening**. Are you going to sleep?
5. Yes, I'm tired. **Good night**.
6. **Good night**. **See you again**.
7. Sure, **See you again**. **Goodbye**.
8. **No problem**, **Goodbye**.

✤ In rural parts of India, it's common to greet someone by touching their feet as a sign of respect, especially if they are older or of higher social status.

दिन 2: आम वाक्यांश

1. नमस्ते, आप कैसे हैं?
2. **हाँ**, मैं ठीक हूँ। और आप?
3. मैं भी ठीक हूँ। **क्षमा कीजिये**, आपका नाम क्या है?
4. मेरा नाम रोहित है। **और** आपका?
5. मैं सीमा हूँ। **शायद** हम पहले मिले हैं?
6. **नहीं**, मुझे नहीं लगता। **कृपया** यह **छोटा** सा उपहार स्वीकार करें।
7. **ठीक है**, धन्यवाद। अलविदा।
8. **बहुत** धन्यवाद, अलविदा।

✤ In Hindi, the verb usually comes at the end of the sentence.

1. namaste, āp kaise haiṁ?
2. **hām̐**, maiṁ ṭhīk hūm̐. aur āp?
3. maiṁ bhī ṭhīk hūm̐. **kṣamā kījiye**, āpkā nām kyā hai?
4. merā nām rohit hai. **aur** āpkā?
5. maiṁ sīmā hūm̐. **śāyad** ham pahle mile haiṁ?
6. **nahīm̐**, mujhe nahīm̐ lagtā. **kṛpayā** yah **choṭā** sā upahār svīkār kareṁ.
7. **ṭhīk hai**, dhanyavād. alavidā.
8. **bahut** dhanyavād, alavidā.

DAY 2: COMMON EXPRESSIONS

1. Hello, how are you?
2. **Yes**, I'm fine. And you?
3. I'm also fine. **Excuse me**, what is your name?
4. My name is Rohit. **And** yours?
5. I'm Seema. **Perhaps** we've met before?
6. **No**, I don't think so. **Please** accept this **small** gift.
7. **Alright**, thank you. Goodbye.
8. **Thank you very much**, goodbye.

✣ The phrase "Guru Dakshina," meaning offering to a teacher, originates from ancient times when students would give a gift to their guru as a token of gratitude and respect.

दिन 3: परिचय संबंधी शब्दावली

1. आपका नाम क्या है?
2. मेरा नाम राज है। और आप?
3. मैं सीमा हूँ। आप कैसे हैं?
4. मैं ठीक हूँ, धन्यवाद! और आप?
5. मैं भी ठीक हूँ। आपकी उम्र क्या है?
6. मेरी उम्र बीस साल है।
7. अच्छा, मैं भी बीस साल की हूँ।
8. बहुत अच्छा!

✤ In Hindi, adjectives change form to agree with the gender and number of the noun they describe.

1. āpkā nām kyā hai?
2. merā nām rāj hai. aur āp?
3. maiṃ sīmā hūm̐. āp kaise haiṃ?
4. maiṃ ṭhīk hūm̐, dhanyavād! aur āp?
5. maiṃ bhī ṭhīk hūm̐. āpkī umr kyā hai?
6. merī umr bīs sāl hai.
7. acchā, maiṃ bhī bīs sāl kī hūm̐.
8. bahut acchā!

DAY 3: INTRODUCTION VOCABULARY

1. What is your name?
2. My name is Raj. And you?
3. I am Seema. How are you?
4. I am fine, thank you! And you?
5. I am also fine. How old are you?
6. I am twenty years old.
7. Oh, I am also twenty years old.
8. Very good!

✣ In traditional Indian academic gatherings, it's customary to start any presentation or speech by lighting a lamp, symbolizing the removal of darkness or ignorance.

दिन 4: व्यक्तिगत जानकारी

1. नमस्ते, आपका नाम क्या है?
2. मेरा नाम सीमा है। आप कहाँ से हैं?
3. मैं दिल्ली से हूँ। आप कहाँ रहते हैं?
4. मैं मुंबई में रहती हूँ। आप क्या करते हैं?
5. मैं शिक्षक हूँ। आपको क्या पसंद है?
6. मुझे संगीत और खेल पसंद हैं। मेरी उम्र बीस साल है।
7. मिलकर अच्छा लगा! अलविदा।
8. अलविदा, आपका दिन शुभ हो। धन्यवाद!

✤ In Hindi, there is no definite article like "the" in English; instead, context and specificity are used to convey definiteness.

1. namaste, āpkā nām kyā hai?
2. merā nām sīmā hai. āp kahām̐ se haiṁ?
3. maiṁ dillī se hūm̐. āp kahām̐ rahte haiṁ?
4. maiṁ mumbaī meṁ rahtī hūm̐. āp kyā karte haiṁ?
5. maiṁ śikṣak hūm̐. āpko kyā pasamd hai?
6. mujhe saṅgīt aur khel pasamd haiṁ. merī umr bīs sāl hai.
7. milkar acchā lagā! alavidā.
8. alavidā, āpkā din śubh ho. dhanyavād!

DAY 4: PERSONAL INFORMATION

1. Hello, what is your name?
2. My name is Seema. Where are you from?
3. I am from Delhi. Where do you live?
4. I live in Mumbai. What do you do?
5. I am a teacher. What do you like?
6. I like music and sports. I am twenty years old.
7. Nice to meet you! Goodbye.
8. Goodbye, have a nice day. Thank you!

✤ In traditional Indian markets, bargaining often leads to the exchange of personal stories, fostering a unique bond between buyer and seller.

दिन 5: सामान्य क्रियाएँ I

1. तुम क्या कर रहे हो? **मैं देख रहा हूँ** टीवी।
2. तुम्हें क्या चाहिए? **मुझे चाहिए** पानी।
3. तुम्हारे पास क्या है? **मेरे पास हैं** किताबें।
4. तुम क्या समझते हो? **मैं समझता हूँ** थोड़ी हिंदी।
5. तुम कहाँ जा रहे हो? **मैं जा रहा हूँ** बाज़ार।
6. तुम क्या खरीदोगे? **मैं खरीदूँगा** सब्जियाँ।
7. तुम क्या दे सकते हो? **मैं दे सकता हूँ** तुम्हें पेन।
8. तुम क्या कर सकते हो? **मैं कर सकता हूँ** गाना।
9. तुम क्या चाहोगे? **मैं चाहूँगा** चाय।

✤ In Hindi, there is no indefinite article like 'a' or 'an' in English; instead, the context of the sentence makes it clear.

1. Tum kya kar rahe ho? Main dekh raha hoon TV.
2. Tumhe kya chahiye? Mujhe chahiye paani.
3. Tumhare paas kya hai? Mere paas hain kitaaben.
4. Tum kya samajhte ho? Main samajhta hoon thodi Hindi.
5. Tum kahan ja rahe ho? Main ja raha hoon bazaar.
6. Tum kya kharidoge? Main kharidoonga sabziyaan.
7. Tum kya de sakte ho? Main de sakta hoon tumhe pen.
8. Tum kya kar sakte ho? Main kar sakta hoon gaana.
9. Tum kya chahoge? Main chahoonga chai.

1. What are you doing? **I am watching** TV.
2. What do you want? **I want** water.
3. What do you have? **I have** books.
4. What do you understand? **I understand** a little Hindi.
5. Where are you going? **I am going** to the market.
6. What will you buy? **I will buy** vegetables.
7. What can you give? **I can give** you a pen.
8. What can you do? **I can** sing.
9. What would you like? **I would like** tea.

✤ In Hindi, the verb for giving respect, "देना" (dena), is used in various forms to show politeness and honor, embedding cultural values of respect directly into the language.

दिन 6: पेय

1. आपका नाम क्या है?
2. मेरा नाम राज है। आप क्या पीना चाहते हैं?
3. मुझे चाय पसंद है। और आप?
4. मैं कॉफी पीना पसंद करता हूँ।
5. मेरे पास दूध है, चाय बनाऊँ?
6. हाँ, धन्यवाद! और आपकी उम्र कितनी है?
7. मेरी उम्र 25 साल है। क्या आपको शराब या बीयर पसंद है?
8. नहीं, मैं समझता हूँ कि पानी और रस स्वास्थ्य के लिए अच्छे हैं।
9. सही कहा, पानी सबसे अच्छा पेय है।

✤ In Hindi, when talking about beverages, use the pronoun "यह" (this) for something close and "वह" (that) for something far.

1. āpkā nām kyā hai?
2. merā nām rāj hai. āp kyā pīnā cāhte haiṁ?
3. mujhe cāy pasand hai. aur āp?
4. maiṁ kŏphī pīnā pasand karatā hūm̐.
5. mere pās dūdh hai, cāy banāūm̐?
6. hām̐, dhanyavād! aur āpkī umr kitnī hai?
7. merī umr 25 sāl hai. kyā āpko śarāb yā bīyar pasand hai?
8. nahīm̐, maiṁ samajhatā hūm̐ ki pānī aur ras svāsthya ke lie acche haiṁ.
9. sahī kahā, pānī sabse acchā pey hai.

1. What is your name?
2. My name is Raj. What would you like to drink?
3. I like tea. And you?
4. I prefer coffee.
5. I have milk, shall I make tea?
6. Yes, thank you! And how old are you?
7. I prefer to drink coffee.

✣ In ancient India, "Soma" was a sacred drink believed to connect drinkers with the divine.

Important Reminder Before Starting Lesson 7

* * *

Congratulations on your progress so far! You are about to embark on a crucial stage of your learning: Phase No. 2.

Please follow these instructions starting from lesson 7:

- For each lesson from No. 7 onward, first translate the text of that lesson (No. 7, No. 8, etc.) from the target language into English.
- Then, go back 6 lessons and translate the English version of that lesson's text from English back into the target language, without referring to the original text.
- Compare your translation with the original text of that lesson and adjust if necessary.
- Read the original text of that lesson out loud, while listening to the audio.

This new phase is designed to activate the vocabulary you have already assimilated. Keep up the momentum and enjoy this enriching new phase of your learning!

दिन संख्या ७: वर्णनात्मक विशेषण I

1. तुम कहाँ से हो?
2. मैं दिल्ली से हूँ।
3. तुम क्या करते हो?
4. मैं शिक्षक हूँ।
5. तुम्हें क्या पसंद है?
6. मुझे ठंडा पानी और गर्म चाय पसंद है।
7. तुम कहाँ रहते हो?
8. मैं एक छोटे शहर में रहता हूँ।
9. मिलकर अच्छा लगा!
10. आपका दिन शुभ हो।

✤ In Hindi, adjectives do not change when they are used as adverbs; they remain in their basic form.

1. tum kahām̐ se ho?
2. maiṃ dillī se hūm̐.
3. tum kyā karate ho?
4. maiṃ śikṣak hūm̐.
5. tumhem̐ kyā pasam̐d hai?
6. mujhe ṭhaṇḍā pānī aur garm cāy pasam̐d hai.
7. tum kahām̐ rahate ho?
8. maiṃ ek choṭe śahar meṃ rahatā hūm̐.
9. milkar acchā lagā!
10. āpakā din śubh ho.

DAY 7: DESCRIPTIVE ADJECTIVES I

1. Where are you from?
2. I am from Delhi.
3. What do you do?
4. I am a teacher.
5. What do you like?
6. I like cold water and hot tea.
7. Where do you live?
8. I live in a small town.
9. Nice to meet you!
10. Have a good day.

✤ In Hindi literature, "sundar" (beautiful) often describes not just physical beauty, but the beauty of one's soul and actions.

दिन 8: स्थान और दिशाएँ I

1. **यहाँ** क्या है?
2. **वहाँ** एक पार्क है।
3. पार्क **दूर** है या **नज़दीक**?
4. बहुत **नज़दीक**। **सीधे** जाओ और फिर **बाएँ** मुड़ो।
5. **दाएँ** नहीं?
6. नहीं, **बाएँ**। **उधर** से **अंदर** जाओ।
7. **इधर** से भी जा सकते हैं?
8. हाँ, पर **इधर** से **दूर** है।
9. समझ गया, धन्यवाद।

✤ In Hindi, to indicate location, we often use the preposition "में" (mein) after the noun, meaning "in" or "at".

1. **yahā̃** kyā hai?
2. **vahā̃** ek pārk hai.
3. pārk **dūr** hai yā **nazdīk**?
4. bahut **nazdīk**. **sīdhe** jāo aur phir **bāẽ** muḍo.
5. **dāẽ** nahī̃?
6. nahī̃, **bāẽ**. **udhar** se **andar** jāo.
7. **idhar** se bhī jā sakte haī̃?
8. hā̃, par **idhar** se **dūr** hai.
9. samajh gayā, dhanyavād.

DAY 8: LOCATION AND DIRECTIONS I

1. **What** is here?
2. **There** is a park.
3. Is the park **far** or **near**?
4. Very **near**. Go **straight** and then turn **left**.
5. Not **right**?
6. No, **left**. Go **in** from **there**.
7. Can we also go from **here**?
8. Yes, but it's **farther** from **here**.
9. Understood, thank you.

✤ The Taj Mahal, a symbol of love, was built by Emperor Shah Jahan in memory of his wife Mumtaz Mahal and it took over 20,000 workers and 1,000 elephants to complete.

दिन 9: स्थान और दिशाएँ II

1. **ऊपर** क्या है?
2. **नीचे** कुछ नहीं है।
3. **पीछे** क्या है?
4. **बगल में** एक कैफे है।
5. **बाएँ मुड़ें** या **दाएँ मुड़ें**?
6. **बाएँ मुड़ें, फिर यहाँ रुकें।**
7. वहाँ चाय मिलेगी या कॉफ़ी?
8. चाय, कॉफ़ी, बीयर, पानी, सोडा सब मिलेगा।
9. अच्छा, चलो **बाएँ** मुड़ते हैं।

✣ In Hindi, to combine sentences about locations or directions, we use conjunctions like "और" (and), "लेकिन" (but), and "या" (or).

1. **Ūpara** kyā hai?
2. **Nīce** kucha nahīṁ hai.
3. **Pīche** kyā hai?
4. **Bagala meṁ** eka kaiphē hai.
5. **Bā'eṁ muṛeṁ** yā **Dā'eṁ muṛeṁ**?
6. **Bā'eṁ muṛeṁ, phira Yahām̐ rukeṁ.**
7. Vahām̐ cāya milegī yā kāphī?
8. Cāya, kāphī, bīyara, pānī, sōḍā saba milegā.
9. Acchā, calo **Bā'eṁ** muṛate haiṁ.

1. **Above** what is there?
2. **Below** there is nothing.
3. **Behind** what is there?
4. **Next to it** there is a cafe.
5. **Turn left** or **turn right**?
6. **Turn left**, then **stop here**.
7. Will there be tea or coffee there?
8. Tea, coffee, beer, water, soda, everything is available.
9. Alright, let's **turn left**.

✣ The Taj Mahal was built by Emperor Shah Jahan as a mausoleum for his wife, Mumtaz Mahal, symbolizing eternal love.

दिन 10: प्रश्न

1. कौन?
2. यहाँ कौन है?
3. कहाँ?
4. क्या?
5. क्या आवाज है?
6. कैसे?
7. क्यों?
8. कब?
9. कितना?
10. कौन सा?

✤ In Hindi, to turn a statement into a question, often you just need to add "क्या" at the beginning of the sentence.

1. Kaun?
2. Yahan kaun hai?
3. Kahan?
4. Kya?
5. Kya awaz hai?
6. Kaise?
7. Kyon?
8. Kab?
9. Kitna?
10. Kaun sa?

DAY 10: QUESTIONS

1. Who?
2. Who's there?
3. Where?
4. What?
5. What's that sound?
6. How?
7. Why?
8. When?
9. How much?
10. Which one?

✤ In traditional Indian classrooms, students often show respect by not questioning their teachers, reflecting a deep-rooted cultural reverence for educators.

CHALLENGE NO. 1

CHOOSE A THEME AND CREATE A COLLAGE OF PHOTOS OR IMAGES, NOTING THE CORRESPONDING WORD IN HINDI.

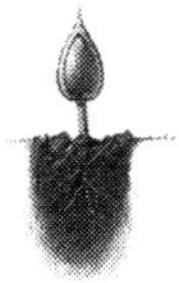

"संघर्ष में आदमी अकेला होता है, सफलता में दुनिया उसके साथ होती है।"

"In struggle, a person is alone; in success, the world is with him."

दिन 11: दिन और समय

1. **आज** क्या समय है?
2. **अभी** दोपहर के तीन **बजे** हैं।
3. **कल** आप कहाँ थे?
4. मैं यहाँ था।
5. **परसों** आप क्या करेंगे?
6. मैं दोस्त के साथ फिल्म देखूंगा।
7. **समय** कितना होता है?
8. **समय सेकंड**, **मिनट, और घंटे** में होता है।
9. **कल** कितने बजे मिलेंगे?
10. **कल** शाम के पांच बजे।

✤ In Hindi, to say "It is 3 o'clock," you simply say "यह तीन बजे हैं।" (Yah teen baje hain.)

1. **āja** kyā samaya hai?
2. **abhī** dophara ke tīna **baje** haiṃ.
3. **kala** āpa kahām̐ the?
4. maiṃ yahām̐ thā.
5. **parasoṃ** āpa kyā kareṃge?
6. maiṃ dosta ke sātha philma dekhūṃgā.
7. **samaya** kitnā hotā hai?
8. **samaya sekaṇḍa**, **minaṭa, aura ghaṇṭe** meṃ hotā hai.
9. **kala** kitane baje mileṃge?
10. **kala** śāma ke pām̐ca baje.

1. **Today** what time is it?
2. **It's** three in the afternoon **now**.
3. **Yesterday** where were you?
4. I was here.
5. **The day after tomorrow** what will you do?
6. I will watch a movie with a friend.
7. **Time** is measured in what?
8. **Time** is in **seconds, minutes, and hours**.
9. **Tomorrow** at what time shall we meet?
10. **Tomorrow** at five in the evening.

✤ In ancient India, time was conceptualized as a vast cosmic cycle, endlessly repeating in a concept known as "Kalachakra."

दिन 12: सप्ताह के दिन

1. आज कौन सा दिन है?
2. आज सोमवार है।
3. कल मंगलवार होगा?
4. हाँ, कल मंगलवार होगा।
5. और परसों?
6. परसों बुधवार होगा।
7. सप्ताहांत में क्या करेंगे?
8. शनिवार और रविवार को आराम करेंगे।
9. ठीक है, शुक्रवार को मिलते हैं।

✤ In Hindi, the days of the week are always masculine, so when they are the subject, verbs and adjectives agree with them in the masculine form.

1. āja kauna sā dina hai?
2. āja somavāra hai.
3. kala maṅgalavāra hogā?
4. hām̐, kala maṅgalavāra hogā.
5. aura parasoṁ?
6. parasoṁ budhavāra hogā.
7. saptāhānta mẽ kyā kareṅge?
8. śanivāra aura ravivāra ko ārāma kareṅge.
9. ṭhīka hai, śukravāra ko milate haiṁ.

DAY 12: DAYS OF THE WEEK

1. What day is it today?
2. Today is Monday.
3. Will it be Tuesday tomorrow?
4. Yes, it will be Tuesday tomorrow.
5. And the day after tomorrow?
6. The day after tomorrow will be Wednesday.
7. What shall we do on the weekend?
8. We will rest on Saturday and Sunday.
9. Alright, let's meet on Friday.

✤ In Hindi, the days of the week are named after the planets and celestial bodies, reflecting ancient astrological beliefs.

दिन 13: परिवार I

1. **माँ**, आज **बुधवार** है, **पिता** कहाँ हैं?
2. **पिता** दफ्तर गए हैं।
3. **भाई** और **बहन** स्कूल क्यों नहीं गए?
4. आज उनकी छुट्टी है।
5. **माता-पिता** के साथ **बच्चे** पार्क कब जाएंगे?
6. शाम को।
7. **दादा-दादी** कैसे हैं?
8. वे अच्छे हैं, धन्यवाद!
9. **पति** और **पत्नी** आज शाम क्या करेंगे?
10. वे फिल्म देखने जाएंगे।

✣ In Hindi, the direct object of a verb usually comes before the verb and agrees in gender and number with it.

1. **mām̐**, āja **budhavāra** hai, **pitā** kahām̐ haim̐?
2. **pitā** daftara ga'e haim̐.
3. **bhā'ī** aura **bahana** skūla kyoṁ nahīm̐ ga'e?
4. āja unakī chuṭṭī hai.
5. **mātā-pitā** ke sātha **bacce** pārka kaba jā'em̐ge?
6. śāma ko.
7. **dādā-dādī** kaise haim̐?
8. ve acche haim̐, dhanyavāda!
9. **pati** aura **patnī** āja śāma kyā karem̐ge?
10. ve philm dekhane jā'em̐ge.

DAY 13: FAMILY I

1. **Mother**, today is **Wednesday**, where is **father**?
2. **Father** has gone to the office.
3. Why didn't **brother** and **sister** go to school?
4. They have a holiday today.
5. When will the **children** go to the park with **parents**?
6. In the evening.
7. How are **grandfather** and **grandmother**?
8. They are fine, thank you!
9. What will **husband** and **wife** do this evening?
10. They will go to watch a movie.

✤ In traditional Indian families, it's common for three or more generations to live under one roof, fostering a deep sense of unity and interdependence.

दिन 14: परिवार II

1. तुम कहाँ से हो?
2. मैं दिल्ली से हूँ।
3. तुम्हारा परिवार कैसा है?
4. मेरे परिवार में माँ, पिता, एक भाई और एक बहन हैं।
5. तुम्हारे चचेरे भाई या चचेरी बहन हैं?
6. हाँ, मेरे दो चचेरे भाई और एक चचेरी बहन हैं।
7. तुम्हारे चाचा और चाची कैसे हैं?
8. वे अच्छे हैं। चाचा एक सहकर्मी हैं और चाची घर पर रहती हैं।
9. और तुम्हारे भतीजे और भतीजी?
10. वे स्कूल जाते हैं। मिलकर अच्छा लगा!
11. आपका दिन शुभ हो।

✤ In Hindi, to indicate an indirect object, we often use the postposition 'को' (ko) after the noun.

1. tum kahām̐ se ho?
2. maiṃ dillī se hūm̐.
3. tumhārā parivār kaisā hai?
4. mere parivār meṃ mām̐, pitā, ek bhāī aur ek bahin haim̐.
5. tumhāre cacere bhāī yā cacarī bahin haim̐?
6. hām̐, mere do cacere bhāī aur ek cacarī bahin haim̐.
7. tumhāre cācā aur cācī kaise haim̐?
8. ve acche haim̐. cācā ek sahakarmī haim̐ aur cācī ghar par rahtī haim̐.
9. aur tumhāre bhatīje aur bhatījī?
10. ve skūl jāte haim̐. milkar acchā lagā!
11. āpkā din śubh ho.

DAY 14: FAMILY II

1. Where are you from?
2. I am from Delhi.
3. How is your family?
4. In my family, there is a mother, father, one brother, and one sister.
5. Do you have any cousins?
6. Yes, I have two male cousins and one female cousin.
7. How are your uncle and aunt?
8. They are good. Uncle is a colleague, and aunt stays at home.
9. And your nephews and nieces?
10. They go to school. It was nice meeting you!
11. Have a nice day.

✣ In India, Diwali, the Festival of Lights, sees families coming together to light diyas, symbolizing the victory of light over darkness and good over evil.

दिन 15: 1 से 10 तक की संख्याएँ

1. **एक** चचेरा भाई है मेरे पास।
2. **दो** चचेरी बहनें हैं।
3. **तीन** चाची हैं मेरी।
4. **चार** दिन सोमवार से गुरुवार तक मैं स्कूल जाता हूँ।
5. **पांच** रुपये की मुझे जरूरत है।
6. **छह** पेंसिलें मेरे पास हैं।
7. **सात** बजे मैं खेलने जाऊंगा।
8. **आठ** बजे मुझे पता है चाचा आएंगे।
9. **नौ** और **दस** साल के भतीजे हैं मेरे।

✤ In Hindi, when using numbers from 1 to 10 in present tense sentences, the verb agrees with the subject's number and gender, not with the numeral.

1. **ek** cacērā bhā'ī hai mere pās.
2. **do** cacērī bahanēṁ haiṁ.
3. **tīn** cācī haiṁ merī.
4. **cār** din somavār se guruvar tak ma͡ī skūl jātā hūm̐.
5. **pām̐c** rupaye kī mujhe jarūrat hai.
6. **chaḥ** pensileṁ mere pās haiṁ.
7. **sāt** baje ma͡ī khelne jāūm̐gā.
8. **āṭh** baje mujhe patā hai cācā ā'em̐ge.
9. **nau** aur **das** sāl ke bhatīje haiṁ mere.

DAY 15: NUMBERS FROM 1 TO 10

1. **One** cousin brother I have.
2. **Two** cousin sisters I have.
3. **Three** aunts are mine.
4. **Four** days from Monday to Thursday I go to school.
5. **Five** rupees I need.
6. **Six** pencils I have.
7. **Seven** o'clock I will go to play.
8. **Eight** o'clock I know uncle will come.
9. **Nine** and **Ten** years old nephews I have.

✤ In India, the number 13 is often considered lucky, contrasting the Western superstition where it's deemed unlucky.

दिन संख्या 16: 11 से 20 तक की संख्याएँ

1. **ग्यारह** बजे हैं, चाय बनाऊँ?
2. हाँ, और **बारह** बिस्कुट भी ले आना।
3. **तेरह** लोग हैं, पर्याप्त होगा?
4. नहीं, **चौदह** कप चाय बनाओ।
5. **पंद्रह** मिनट में तैयार हो जाएगी।
6. **सोलह** चम्मच चीनी डालना।
7. **सत्रह** नहीं, बहुत मीठा हो जाएगा।
8. **अठारह** चम्मच दूध और डालो।
9. **उन्नीस** लोग आ गए, और चाय बनाओ।
10. **बीस** मिनट और लगेंगे।

✤ In Hindi, numbers from 11 to 20 end with "rah" (रह) when used in the affirmative form, as in "Gyarah" (11) or "Barah" (12).

1. **gyāraha** baje haiṁ, cāya banāūm̐?
2. hām̐, aura **bāraha** biskuṭa bhī le ānā.
3. **teraha** loga haiṁ, paryāpta hogā?
4. nahīṁ, **caudaha** kapa cāya banāo.
5. **panḍraha** minaṭa meṁ taiyāra ho jā'egī.
6. **solaha** cammaca cīnī ḍālanā.
7. **satraha** nahīṁ, bahuta mīṭhā ho jā'egā.
8. **aṭhāraha** cammaca dūdha aura ḍālo.
9. **unnīsa** loga ā gae, aura cāya banāo.
10. **bīsa** minaṭa aura lagem̐ge.

DAY 16: NUMBERS FROM 11 TO 20

1. **Eleven** o'clock, shall I make tea?
2. Yes, and bring **twelve** biscuits too.
3. There are **thirteen** people, will it be enough?
4. No, make **fourteen** cups of tea.
5. It will be ready in **fifteen** minutes.
6. Add **sixteen** spoons of sugar.
7. Not **seventeen**, it will be too sweet.
8. Add **eighteen** more spoons of milk.
9. **Nineteen** people have arrived, make more tea.
10. It will take **twenty** more minutes.

✤ In India, the game "Antakshari," often starting with a specific number, turns any gathering into a lively Bollywood song competition.

1. **बाजार** में चलें, **दुकानें** देखेंगे।
2. हाँ, मुझे **खरीदारी** करनी है। **सेल** है क्या?
3. हाँ, बहुत **छूट** मिल रही है।
4. यह कितना **महंगा** है?
5. नहीं, यह तो बहुत **सस्ता** है।
6. **नकद** देंगे या **क्रेडिट कार्ड** से?
7. मेरे पास **नकद** है।
8. अच्छा है, **नकद** में और **छूट** मिलेगी।
9. चलो फिर, **खरीदारी** शुरू करते हैं।

✤ In Hindi, to make a sentence negative, add "नहीं" (nahīn) before the verb, like "मैं खरीदता नहीं हूँ" (I do not buy).

1. **bāzār** meṁ caleṁ, **dukānen** dekheṁge।
2. hām̐, mujhe **kharīdārī** karnī hai। **sel** hai kyā?
3. hām̐, bahut **chūṭ** mil rahī hai।
4. yah kitnā **mahaṁgā** hai?
5. nahīm̐, yah to bahut **sastā** hai।
6. **nakad** deṁge yā **kreḍiṭ kārḍ** se?
7. mere pās **nakad** hai।
8. acchā hai, **nakad** meṁ aur **chūṭ** milegī।
9. calo phir, **kharīdārī** śurū karte haiṁ।

1. Let's go to the **market**, we'll look at the **shops**.
2. Yes, I need to do some **shopping**. Is there a **sale**?
3. Yes, there's a big **discount** going on.
4. How **expensive** is this?
5. No, this is very **cheap**.
6. Will you pay in **cash** or with a **credit card**?
7. I have **cash**.
8. Good, you'll get an additional **discount** with **cash**.
9. Let's go then, start the **shopping**.

✤ In traditional Indian markets, it's common to start negotiations at half the asking price, blending respect with the art of a good deal.

दिन 18: शॉपिंग II

1. यह जैकेट कितने का है? **मूल्य** तीन हजार रुपये है।
2. और यह धूप का चश्मा? **मूल्य** पांच सौ रुपये है।
3. ट्रायल रूम कहाँ है? वहाँ दाएँ।
4. कैश काउंटर? सीधे आगे।
5. **रसीद** मिलेगी? हाँ, **रसीद** जरूर मिलेगी।
6. **गाड़ी** में सामान रख दूँ? हाँ, और **टोकरी** यहाँ छोड़ दीजिए।

✤ To form a question in Hindi about shopping, start your sentence with "क्या" (kya) for yes/no questions or use question words like "कौन" (kaun) for "who", "क्यों" (kyon) for "why", and "कहाँ" (kahan) for "where".

1. yah jaikeṭa kitanē kā hai? **mūlya** tīna hajāra rupaye hai.
2. aura yaha dhūpa kā caśmā? **mūlya** pāṃca sau rupaye hai.
3. ṭrāyala rūma kahām̐ hai? vahām̐ dāēm̐.
4. kaiśa kā'uṇṭara? sīdhē āgē.
5. **rasīda** milēgī? hām̐, **rasīda** jarūra milēgī.
6. **gāṛī** mēṃ sāmāna rakha dūm̐? hām̐, aura **ṭōkarī** yahām̐ chōṛa dījiē.

1. How much is this jacket? **Price** It is three thousand rupees.
2. And this pair of sunglasses? **Price** Five hundred rupees.
3. Where is the fitting room? Over there to the right.
4. Cash counter? Straight ahead.
5. **Receipt** Will I get one? Yes, you will definitely get a **receipt**.
6. Should I put the items in the **car**? Yes, and please leave the **basket** here.

✤ India's first shopping mall, Spencer Plaza in Chennai, originally started as a department store in 1863.

1. **हवाई अड्डा** जाने के लिए **टैक्सी** कहाँ मिलेगी?
2. यहाँ रुकें, **बस** स्टैंड के बगल में **टैक्सी** स्टैंड है।
3. **रेलवे स्टेशन** के लिए **ट्रेन** कब है?
4. **ट्रेन** हर घंटे है। **कार** से जाना बेहतर है।
5. **हवाई जहाज** की रसीद कहाँ मिलेगी?
6. कैश काउंटर पर।
7. मुझे **साइकिल** चलाना है।
8. **साइकिल** किराए पर यहाँ मिलेगी।
9. और **नाव** की सवारी?
10. नदी के किनारे **नाव** मिलेगी।

✤ In Hindi, a declarative sentence about transport, like "She goes to school by bus," is structured as "वह बस से स्कूल जाती है।"

1. **havāī aḍḍā** jāne ke lie **ṭaiksi** kahām̐ milegī?
2. yahām̐ rukem, **bas** sṭaiṇḍ ke bagal mem **ṭaiksi** sṭaiṇḍ hai.
3. **relve sṭeśan** ke lie **ṭren** kab hai?
4. **ṭren** har ghaṇṭe hai. **kār** se jānā behtar hai.
5. **havāī jahāj** kī rasīd kahām̐ milegī?
6. kaiś kāuṇṭar par.
7. mujhe **saikil** calānā hai.
8. **saikil** kirāe par yahām̐ milegī.
9. aur **nāv** kī savārī?
10. nadī ke kināre **nāv** milegī.

DAY 19: TRANSPORT I

1. Where can I find a **taxi** to go to the **airport**?
2. Stop here, next to the **bus** stand there is a **taxi** stand.
3. When is the **train** for the **railway station**?
4. There is a **train** every hour. It's better to go by **car**.
5. Where can I get the **airplane** ticket?
6. At the cash counter.
7. I want to ride a **bicycle**.
8. You can rent a **bicycle** here.
9. And what about a **boat** ride?
10. You will find a **boat** by the riverbank.

✤ In rural India, camels are not just for desert travel but also serve as mobile libraries, bringing books to remote villages.

दिन 20: परिवहन II

1. क्या आपके पास **टिकट** है?
2. हां, मेरे पास **बोर्डिंग पास** भी है।
3. **प्रस्थान** कब है?
4. दस मिनट में। **आगमन** कब होगा?
5. शाम को। आपका **टर्मिनल** कौन सा है?
6. **टर्मिनल** दो। और **द्वार**?
7. **द्वार** तीन। आपका **सामान** कहाँ है?
8. मेरा **सूटकेस** और **बैकपैक** यहाँ हैं।
9. अच्छा, चलो जल्दी करें, फ्लाइट **विलंबित** नहीं है।

✣ To ask about modes of transport in Hindi, start your sentence with "कौन सा" (which) or "कैसे" (how), for example, "कौन सी बस शहर के लिए जाती है?" (Which bus goes to the city?).

1. kyā āpke pās **ṭikaṭ** hai?
2. hāṁ, mere pās **borḍiṅg pās** bhī hai.
3. **prasthān** kab hai?
4. das minaṭ meṁ. **āgaman** kab hogā?
5. śām ko. āpkā **ṭarminl** kauṁ sā hai?
6. **ṭarminl** do. aur **dvār**?
7. **dvār** tīn. āpkā **sāmān** kahāṁ hai?
8. merā **sūṭkes** aur **baikpaik** yahāṁ haiṁ.
9. achchhā, calo jaldī kareṁ, phlāiṭ **vilambiṭ** nahīṁ hai.

1. Do you have a **ticket**?
2. Yes, I also have a **boarding pass**.
3. When is the **departure**?
4. In ten minutes. When will the **arrival** be?
5. In the evening. Which **terminal** is yours?
6. **Terminal** two. And the **gate**?
7. **Gate** three. Where is your **luggage**?
8. My **suitcase** and **backpack** are here.
9. Alright, let's hurry, the flight is not **delayed**.

✣ India's first passenger train journey covered a distance of 34 kilometers, connecting Mumbai and Thane on April 16, 1853.

CHALLENGE NO. 2

WRITE A SHORT TEXT IN HINDI INTRODUCING YOURSELF AND EXPLAINING WHY YOU ARE LEARNING THIS LANGUAGE.

"ज्ञान वह सूर्य है जो कभी अस्त नहीं होता।"

"Knowledge is that sun which never sets."

दिन 21: स्थान और स्थल I

1. **आज** आप कहाँ जा रहे हैं?
2. **स्कूल** के बाद मैं **बैंक** जाऊंगा।
3. और फिर?
4. **फार्मेसी** से दवाई लेने के बाद **रेस्टोरेंट** में खाना खाऊंगा।
5. **घर** वापस कब आओगे?
6. **अस्पताल** के पास से **पार्क** में टहलने के बाद।
7. मुझे **होटल** के पास **कार्यालय** से एक रसीद लेनी है।
8. मैं तुम्हें **गाड़ी** में छोड़ दूंगा।
9. धन्यवाद! फिर **कल** मिलते हैं।

✣ To give directions or commands about locations in Hindi, use the imperative form of the verb, like "जाओ" (go) or "आओ" (come).

1. **āja** āpa kahām̐ jā rahe haim̐?
2. **skūla** ke bāda main **baim̐ka** jāūm̐gā.
3. aura phira?
4. **phārmesī** se davaī lene ke bāda **resṭoremṭa** mem̐ khānā khāūm̐gā.
5. **ghara** vāpasa kaba āoge?
6. **aspatāla** ke pāsa se **pārka** mem̐ ṭahalane ke bāda.
7. mujhe **hoṭela** ke pāsa **kāryālaya** se eka rasīda lenī hai.
8. main tumhem̐ **gāṛī** mem̐ choṛa dūm̐gā.
9. dhanyavāda! phira **kala** milate haim̐.

1. **Today** where are you going?
2. After **school**, I will go to the **bank**.
3. And then?
4. After picking up medicine from the **pharmacy**, I will eat at a **restaurant**.
5. When will you come back **home**?
6. After walking in the **park** near the **hospital**.
7. I need to pick up a receipt from the **office** near the **hotel**.
8. I will drop you off in the **car**.
9. Thank you! See you **tomorrow**.

✣ India's Taj Mahal, a symbol of love, is cleaned periodically with a traditional mud pack therapy, preserving its white marble glow.

दिन 22: विशेषण II

1. यह **ऊँची** इमारत क्या है?
2. यह एक **बड़ा** होटल है।
3. और वह **नीची** भवन?
4. वह एक **छोटा** स्कूल है।
5. क्या यहाँ पास में कोई **शोरीली** जगह है?
6. हाँ, वहाँ एक **चौड़ा** और **शोरीला** बाज़ार है।
7. मुझे **धीमा** और **शांत** पार्क चाहिए।
8. पार्क तो वहाँ है, **लंबे** पेड़ों के पास।
9. अच्छा, मैं वहाँ **तेज़ी** से चलकर जाऊँगा।

✤ In Hindi, to form an exclamatory sentence with an adjective, place the adjective before the noun and add "कितना/कितनी" (kitna/kitni) for 'how much/many' or 'what a' before the adjective.

1. yah **ū̃cī** imārat kyā hai?
2. yah ek **baṛā** hoṭal hai.
3. aur vah **nīcī** bhavan?
4. vah ek **choṭā** skūl hai.
5. kyā yahām̐ pās meṃ koī **śorīlī** jagah hai?
6. hām̐, vahām̐ ek **cauṛā** aur **śorīlā** bāzār hai.
7. mujhe **dhīmā** aur **śānt** pārk cāhie.
8. pārk to vahām̐ hai, **lambē** peṛom̐ ke pās.
9. acchā, maĩ vahām̐ **tēzī** se calakar jāūm̐gā.

1. What is this **tall** building?
2. It's a **big** hotel.
3. And that **low** building?
4. That's a **small** school.
5. Is there any **noisy** place nearby?
6. Yes, there's a **wide** and **noisy** market there.
7. I want a **quiet** and **peaceful** park.
8. The park is there, near the **tall** trees.
9. Alright, I will walk there **quickly**.

✣ In India, the Valley of Flowers National Park, a UNESCO World Heritage Site, transforms into a vibrant carpet of blossoming flowers every monsoon.

दिन 23: विशेषण III

1. यह बैग **भारी** है या **हल्का**?
2. **हल्का है, लेकिन भरा हुआ** है।
3. मौसम कैसा है?
4. **गर्म** भी है और **ठंडा** भी।
5. यह कुर्सी **कठिन** है या **मुलायम**?
6. बहुत **मुलायम** है।
7. और यह तौलिया?
8. वह **गीला** है, मुझे **सूखा** चाहिए।
9. चलो, **शांत** रहो, मैं अभी लाता हूँ।

✤ In Hindi, to make a sentence negative, add "नहीं" (nahin) before the verb.

1. yah bai̱ga **bhārī** hai yā **halkā**?
2. **halkā hai, lekina bharā hua** hai.
3. mausama kaisā hai?
4. **garam** bhī hai aura **ṭhaṇḍā** bhī.
5. yah kursī **kaṭhina** hai yā **mulāyama**?
6. bahuta **mulāyama** hai.
7. aura yah tauliyā?
8. vaha **gīlā** hai, mujhe **sūkhā** cāhie.
9. calo, **śānta** raho, maiṁ abhī lātā hūm̐.

DAY 23: ADJECTIVES III

1. Is this bag **heavy** or **light**?
2. It's **light**, but it's **full**.
3. How's the weather?
4. It's both **hot** and **cold**.
5. Is this chair **hard** or **soft**?
6. It's very **soft**.
7. And this towel?
8. It's **wet**, I need a **dry** one.
9. Come on, **stay calm**, I'll bring it now.

✤ Hindi poets often use adjectives to paint vivid imagery, making even monsoons dance in their verses.

दिन 24: रंग

1. आज स्कूल में रंगों का दिन है।
2. हाँ, मैंने **नीली** शर्ट पहनी है।
3. मेरी बहन ने **गुलाबी** फ्रॉक पहनी है।
4. मेरा भतीजा **हरी** टी-शर्ट पहनकर आया है।
5. और मेरी चाची **लाल** साड़ी में बहुत सुंदर लग रही हैं।
6. मेरे चाचा ने **काला** सूट पहना है।
7. स्कूल के बाहर **पीले** फूल भी खिले हैं।
8. हाँ, और पार्क में **भूरा** पत्थर भी है।
9. अच्छा, चलो अब **सफेद** और **धूसर** रंग ढूंढते हैं।

✤ In Hindi, the spelling of color names changes based on gender; for masculine nouns, use "ा" (a) at the end, and for feminine nouns, use "ी" (i).

1. āja skūl mẽ raṅgõ kā din hai.
2. hā̃, mainne **nīlī** śarṭ pahanī hai.
3. merī bahan ne **gulābī** frok pahanī hai.
4. merā bhatījā **harī** ṭī-śarṭ pahankar āyā hai.
5. aur merī cācī **lāl** sāṛī mẽ bahut sundar lag rahī haiṁ̐.
6. mere cācā ne **kālā** sūṭ pahanā hai.
7. skūl ke bāhar **pīle** phūl bhī khile haiṁ̐.
8. hā̃, aur pārk mẽ **bhūrā** patthar bhī hai.
9. acchā, calo ab **saphed** aur **dhūsar** raṅg ḍhūṅḍhte haiṁ̐.

DAY 24: COLORS

1. Today is the day of colors at school.
2. Yes, I am wearing a **blue** shirt.
3. My sister is wearing a **pink** frock.
4. My nephew has come wearing a **green** T-shirt.
5. And my aunt looks very beautiful in a **red** saree.
6. My uncle is wearing a **black** suit.
7. Outside the school, **yellow** flowers have also bloomed.
8. Yes, and there is also a **brown** stone in the park.
9. Alright, let's now look for **white** and **gray** colors.

✤ In Hindi culture, saffron represents courage and sacrifice, central to the national flag's symbolism.

दिन 25: इलेक्ट्रॉनिक्स और प्रौद्योगिकी I

1. नमस्ते, तुम्हारा **स्मार्टफोन** बड़ा है या छोटा?
2. नमस्ते, मेरा **स्मार्टफोन** छोटा है। और तुम्हारा **लैपटॉप**?
3. मेरा **लैपटॉप** बड़ा और नीला है। तुम **ईमेल** भेजते हो?
4. हाँ, मैं **ईमेल** भेजता हूँ। तुम **वाई-फाई** से जुड़े हो?
5. हाँ, मेरा **कंप्यूटर वाई-फाई** से जुड़ा है। तुम **सोशल मीडिया** पर हो?
6. नहीं, मैं **एप्लिकेशन डाउनलोड करना** पसंद करता हूँ।
7. अच्छा, तुम कौन सा **ब्राउज़र** इस्तेमाल करते हो?
8. मैं **इंटरनेट एक्सप्लोरर** इस्तेमाल करता हूँ। अलविदा।
9. अलविदा।

✤ In Hindi, we use full stops (।) at the end of sentences, just like in English, but the symbol looks different and is called a 'poorna viram'.

1. Namaste, tumhārā **smārtaphōna** baṛā hai yā choṭā?
2. Namaste, merā **smārtaphōna** choṭā hai. Aur tumhārā **laipaṭôpa**?
3. Merā **laipaṭôpa** baṛā aur nīlā hai. Tum **īmela** bhejate ho?
4. Hām̐, maiṁ **īmela** bhejatā hūm̐. Tum **vāī-phāī** se juṛe ho?
5. Hām̐, merā **kampyūṭara vāī-phāī** se juṛā hai. Tum **sōśala mīḍiyā** para ho?
6. Nahīm̐, maiṁ **aplīkeśana ḍāunalōḍa karanā** pasanda karatā hūm̐.
7. Acchā, tum kaun sā **brauzara** istemāla karate ho?
8. Maiṁ **inṭaranēṭa eksaplorara** istemāla karatā hūm̐. Alavidā.
9. Alavidā.

1. Hello, is your **smartphone** big or small?
2. Hello, my **smartphone** is small. And your **laptop**?
3. My **laptop** is big and blue. Do you send **emails**?
4. Yes, I send **emails**. Are you connected to **Wi-Fi**?
5. Yes, my **computer** is connected to **Wi-Fi**. Are you on **social media**?
6. No, I prefer **downloading applications**.
7. Okay, which **browser** do you use?
8. I use **Internet Explorer**. Goodbye.
9. Goodbye.

✣ India invented the game of chess, originally called "Chaturanga," over 1,500 years ago.

दिन 26: महीने और मौसम

1. **जनवरी** में मौसम कैसा होता है? बहुत **ठंडा** होता है।
2. **फरवरी** में भी? हां, पर **फरवरी** में थोड़ा कम।
3. **मार्च** और **अप्रैल** में? **मार्च** में **शांत** और **अप्रैल** में **गर्म** होने लगता है।
4. **मई** और **जून**? बहुत **गर्म**।
5. **जुलाई** से **सितंबर** तक? बारिश होती है, मौसम **मुलायम** हो जाता है।
6. **अक्टूबर** में? **ठंडा** शुरू होता है।

✤ In Hindi, to convert a sentence about months or seasons into the past tense, often the verb at the end changes, for example, "बरसात आती है" (The rain comes) becomes "बरसात आई थी" (The rain had come).

1. **janavarī** mẽ mausam kaisā hotā hai? bahut **ṭhaṇḍā** hotā hai।
2. **pharavarī** mẽ bhī? hāṃ, par **pharavarī** mẽ thoṛā kam।
3. **mārca** aur **apra'il** mẽ? **mārca** mẽ **śānta** aur **apra'il** mẽ **garam** hone lagtā hai।
4. **ma'ī** aur **jūna**? bahut **garam**।
5. **julā'ī** se **sitambara** taka? bāriś hotī hai, mausam **mulāyam** ho jātā hai।
6. **akṭūbara** mẽ? **ṭhaṇḍā** śurū hotā hai।

1. **January** What's the weather like? It's very **cold**.
2. **February** as well? Yes, but a bit less in **February**.
3. **March and April**? **March** is **calm**, and it starts getting **warm** in **April**.
4. **May and June**? Very **hot**.
5. From **July** to **September**? It rains, the weather becomes **soft**.
6. **October**? It starts getting **cold**.

✣ In India, the festival of Holi, celebrated in spring, involves people throwing colored powders at each other, symbolizing the victory of good over evil and the arrival of spring.

दिन 27: महीनों और मौसमों से परे

1. **नवंबर** में **मौसम** कैसा है?
2. **पतझड़** होता है, थोड़ी **धूप** और थोड़ी **बारिश** होती है।
3. **दिसंबर** और **जनवरी** में?
4. **सर्दी** बहुत होती है।
5. **फरवरी** में **मौसम** का **पूर्वानुमान** क्या है?
6. **सर्दी** कम हो जाती है, **वसंत** आता है।
7. **गर्मी** कब शुरू होती है?
8. **मार्च** से **मई** तक **गर्मी** रहती है।
9. धन्यवाद!

✤ In Hindi, to form the future tense, add "गा" (for masculine singular), "गी" (for feminine singular), and "गे" (for plural) at the end of the verb root.

1. **navaṁbara** mẽ **mausama** kaisā hai?
2. **patajhaṛa** hotā hai, thoṛī **dhūpa** aura thoṛī **bāriśa** hotī hai.
3. **disambara** aura **janavarī** mẽ?
4. **sardī** bahuta hotī hai.
5. **pharavarī** mẽ **mausama** kā **pūrvānumāna** kyā hai?
6. **sardī** kama ho jātī hai, **vasanta** ātā hai.
7. **garmī** kaba śurū hotī hai?
8. **mārca** sē **maī** taka **garmī** rahatī hai.
9. dhanyavāda!

1. What is the **weather** like in **November**?
2. There is **autumn**, with a bit of **sunshine** and a bit of **rain**.
3. And in **December** and **January**?
4. It's very **cold**.
5. What is the **weather forecast** for **February**?
6. The **cold** lessens, **spring** arrives.
7. When does the **heat** start?
8. **Heat** persists from **March** to **May**.
9. Thank you!

✣ In India, the arrival of spring is celebrated with the vibrant festival of Holi, where people throw colored powders at each other.

दिन 28: भावनाएँ I

1. तुम कहाँ से हो?
2. मैं दिल्ली से हूँ।
3. तुम क्या करते हो?
4. मैं छात्र हूँ।
5. तुम्हें क्या पसंद है?
6. मुझे पढ़ाई और गाने पसंद हैं।
7. तुम कहाँ रहते हो?
8. मैं मुंबई में रहता हूँ।
9. मिलकर अच्छा लगा!
10. आपका दिन शुभ हो।

✤ In Hindi, the indicative mood is used to express factual statements, questions, or opinions, as if indicating a fact or reality.

1. tuma kahām̐ se ho?
2. maiṃ dillī se hūm̐.
3. tuma kyā karate ho?
4. maiṃ chātra hūm̐.
5. tumhem̐ kyā pasam̐da hai?
6. mujhe paṛhāī aura gāne pasam̐da haim̐.
7. tuma kahām̐ rahate ho?
8. maiṃ mum̐baī mem̐ rahatā hūm̐.
9. milakara acchā lagā!
10. āpakā dina śubha ho.

DAY 28: FEELINGS I

1. Where are you from?
2. I am from Delhi.
3. What do you do?
4. I am a student.
5. What do you like?
6. I like studying and singing.
7. Where do you live?
8. I live in Mumbai.
9. Nice to meet you!
10. Have a good day.

✤ In traditional Indian weddings, the bride's departure is marked by the "Vidaai" ceremony, where her tears symbolize both sorrow for leaving her family and joy towards embracing a new life.

दिन 29: भावनाएँ II

1. तुम तनावग्रस्त क्यों हो?
2. मैं भ्रमित और चिंतित हूँ, मुझे रेलवे स्टेशन जाना है और मेरे पास टैक्सी नहीं है।
3. मैं समझता हूँ, तुम नाराज न हो। मैं तुम्हें अपनी कार से ले चलूंगा।
4. सच में? तुम मुझे डरा हुआ नहीं देखना चाहते?
5. हाँ, मैं तुमसे प्यार करता हूँ और मुझे तुम्हारी याद आती है जब तुम उदास होते हो।
6. अब मैं प्रसन्न हूँ, तुम मेरे अच्छे दोस्त हो।
7. मैं मजाक कर रहा हूँ, मैं खुश हूँ कि तुम प्रसन्न हो।

✤ In Hindi, the imperative mood is used to give commands or make requests, often ending with "o" (ओ) for respect or "e" (ए) for informal situations.

1. tuma tanāvagrasta kyoṁ ho?
2. maiṁ bhramita aura ciṁtita hūm̐, mujhe relave sṭeśana jānā hai aura mere pāsa ṭaiksi nahīṁ hai.
3. maiṁ samajhatā hūm̐, tuma nārāja na ho. maiṁ tumheṁ apanī kāra se le calūm̐gā.
4. saca meṁ? tuma mujhe ḍarā huā nahīṁ dekhanā cāhate?
5. hām̐, maiṁ tumase pyāra karatā hūm̐ aura mujhe tumhārī yāda ātī hai jaba tuma udāsa hote ho.
6. aba maiṁ prasanna hūm̐, tuma mere acche dost ho.
7. maiṁ majāka karahā hūm̐, maiṁ khuśa hūm̐ ki tuma prasanna ho.

DAY 29: FEELINGS II

1. Why are you stressed?
2. I'm confused and worried, I need to go to the railway station and I don't have a taxi.
3. I understand, don't be upset. I'll take you in my car.
4. Really? You don't want to see me scared?
5. Yes, I love you and I miss you when you're sad.
6. Now I'm happy, you're a good friend.
7. I'm joking, I'm happy that you're happy.

✤ The Taj Mahal, often considered a poetic monument in marble, was built by Emperor Shah Jahan out of love for his wife Mumtaz Mahal.

दिन 30: शरीर के अंग I 🖋

1. **सिर** में दर्द है।
2. **बाल** बहुत उलझे हुए हैं।
3. **आँख** से पानी आ रहा है।
4. **कान** में कुछ सुनाई नहीं दे रहा है।
5. **नाक** बंद है, सर्दी लग गई है।
6. **मुँह** से बदबू आ रही है।
7. **दांत** में दर्द हो रहा है।
8. **हाथ** और **बाजू** में तनाव है।
9. **पैर** में मोच आ गई है।

❖ In Hindi, when talking about body parts in a wish or hypothetical situation, we use the subjunctive mood by adding "ए" to the verb, as in "काश मेरे हाथ लंबे होते।" (I wish my arms were longer.)

1. **sira** mẽ dard hai.
2. **bāla** bahut uljhe hue hã̄.
3. **ām̐kha** se pānī ā rahā hai.
4. **kāna** mẽ kucha sunāī nahī̃ de rahā hai.
5. **nāka** band hai, sardī lag gaī hai.
6. **mum̐ha** se badbū ā rahī hai.
7. **dām̐ta** mẽ dard ho rahā hai.
8. **hātha** aura **bājū** mẽ tanāv hai.
9. **paira** mẽ moc ā gaī hai.

DAY 30: BODY PARTS I

1. **Head** is hurting.
2. **Hair** is very tangled.
3. **Eye** is watering.
4. **Ear** is not hearing anything.
5. **Nose** is blocked, caught a cold.
6. **Mouth** is smelling bad.
7. **Tooth** is in pain.
8. **Hand** and **arm** are tense.
9. **Leg** is sprained.

✣ In ancient India, beauty was considered a reflection of inner virtue and wisdom, transcending physical appearance.

CHALLENGE NO. 3

CHOOSE A SHORT ARTICLE IN A HINDI NEWSPAPER AND TRANSLATE IT INTO ENGLISH.

"बोली एक अमृत है, जो सब कुछ सुधार सकती है।"

"Speech is nectar, which can mend everything."

दिन 31: शरीर के अंग II

1. आज पार्क में बहुत आराम से हवा चल रही है।
2. हां, मेरे पैरों और घुटनों को भी आराम मिल रहा है।
3. तुम्हारी उंगली कैसी है?
4. अब ठीक है। परसों गर्दन में दर्द था।
5. ओह! तुम अस्पताल गए थे?
6. नहीं, घर पर ही आराम किया।
7. अच्छा किया। मेरी पीठ में भी दर्द हो रहा था।
8. तुम गर्म पानी से नहाओ, आराम मिलेगा।
9. हां, वह बहुत अच्छा उपाय है।

✤ If you were to touch your head (सिर) in Hindi, you would say, "If I touch my head, it feels cold."

1. āja pārka mẽ bahuta ārāma sē havā cala rahī hai.
2. hā̃, mērē pairõ aura ghuṭnõ kō bhī ārāma mila rahā hai.
3. tumhārī uṅgalī kaisī hai?
4. aba ṭhīka hai. parasõ gardana mẽ darda thā.
5. ōh! tuma aspatāla gaē thē?
6. nahī̃, ghara para hī ārāma kiyā.
7. acchā kiyā. mērī pīṭha mẽ bhī darda hō rahā thā.
8. tuma garma pānī sē nahā'ō, ārāma milēgā.
9. hā̃, vaha bahuta acchā upāya hai.

DAY 31: BODY PARTS II

1. The breeze in the park is very soothing today.
2. Yes, my legs and knees are also getting some relief.
3. How is your finger doing?
4. It's better now. Had a neck pain the day before yesterday.
5. Oh! Did you go to the hospital?
6. No, just rested at home.
7. That's good. I've been having some back pain as well.
8. You should take a hot bath, it will help.
9. Yes, that's a very good remedy.

✤ In traditional Indian Kathak dance, dancers often tell epic tales through intricate footwork and expressive facial gestures.

दिन 32: समय और कैलेंडर

1. आज कौन सा दिन है?
2. आज बुधवार है।
3. इस सप्ताह के अंत में क्या करना है?
4. कैलेंडर देखो, समय सारिणी बनानी है।
5. इस महीने कितने दिन हैं?
6. तीस दिन हैं।
7. और इस साल?
8. इस साल तीन सौ पैंसठ दिन हैं।
9. अच्छा, मैं घंटे और मिनट देखकर समय सारिणी बनाऊंगा।

✤ In Hindi, to express an action in the active voice related to time and calendar, the subject performing the action comes first, followed by the verb.

1. āja kauna sā dina hai?
2. āja budhavāra hai.
3. isa saptāha kē anta mēṁ kyā karanā hai?
4. kailēṇḍara dēkhō, samaya sāriṇī banānī hai.
5. isa mahīnē kitnē dina haiṁ?
6. tīsa dina haiṁ.
7. aura isa sāla?
8. isa sāla tīna sau paiṁsāṭha dina haiṁ.
9. acchā, maiṁ ghaṁṭē aura minaṭa dēkhakara samaya sāriṇī banā'ūṁgā.

DAY 32: TIME AND CALENDAR

1. What day is it today?
2. Today is Wednesday.
3. What are we doing at the end of this week?
4. Check the calendar, we need to make a schedule.
5. How many days are there in this month?
6. There are thirty days.
7. And this year?
8. This year has three hundred sixty-five days.
9. Okay, I will make a schedule by looking at the hours and minutes.

✤ India's national calendar, the Saka Calendar, was adopted in 1957 and is used alongside the Gregorian calendar for official purposes.

दिन 32: समय और कैलेंडर

1. आज कौन सा दिन है?
2. आज बुधवार है।
3. इस सप्ताह के अंत में क्या करना है?
4. कैलेंडर देखो, समय सारिणी बनानी है।
5. इस महीने कितने दिन हैं?
6. तीस दिन हैं।
7. और इस साल?
8. इस साल तीन सौ पैंसठ दिन हैं।
9. अच्छा, मैं घंटे और मिनट देखकर समय सारिणी बनाऊंगा।

✤ In Hindi, to express an action in the active voice related to time and calendar, the subject performing the action comes first, followed by the verb.

1. āja kauna sā dina hai?
2. āja budhavāra hai.
3. isa saptāha kē anta mēṁ kyā karanā hai?
4. kailēṇḍara dēkhō, samaya sāriṇī banānī hai.
5. isa mahīnē kitnē dina haiṁ?
6. tīsa dina haiṁ.
7. aura isa sāla?
8. isa sāla tīna sau paiṁsāṭha dina haiṁ.
9. acchā, maiṁ ghaṁṭē aura minaṭa dēkhakara samaya sāriṇī banā'ūṁgā.

DAY 32: TIME AND CALENDAR

1. What day is it today?
2. Today is Wednesday.
3. What are we doing at the end of this week?
4. Check the calendar, we need to make a schedule.
5. How many days are there in this month?
6. There are thirty days.
7. And this year?
8. This year has three hundred sixty-five days.
9. Okay, I will make a schedule by looking at the hours and minutes.

✣ India's national calendar, the Saka Calendar, was adopted in 1957 and is used alongside the Gregorian calendar for official purposes.

दिन 33: भोजन I

1. **चाय** पिएंगे या **कॉफ़ी**?
2. **चाय** अच्छी है। **बीयर** नहीं पीता।
3. **मांस** खाएंगे या **सब्ज़ियां**?
4. **सब्ज़ियां और फल** पसंद हैं।
5. **रोटी** या **चावल**?
6. **रोटी** गर्म हो तो अच्छी है।
7. **पास्ता और अंडा** कैसा रहेगा?
8. हां, **पास्ता** मुलायम और **अंडा** गर्म हो।
9. ठीक है, यहां रुको, मैं अभी बनाता हूं।

✤ In Hindi, to form the passive voice for sentences about food, you often use the verb "खाया जाता है" (is eaten) after the food item.

1. **cāy** piyeṅge yā **kŏphī**?
2. **cāy** acchī hai. **bīyar** nahīṁ pītā.
3. **māṁs** khāyeṅge yā **sabzīyāṁ**?
4. **sabzīyāṁ aur phal** pasand haiṁ.
5. **roṭī** yā **cāval**?
6. **roṭī** garam ho to acchī hai.
7. **pāstā aur aṇḍā** kaisā rahegā?
8. hāṁ, **pāstā** mulāyam aur **aṇḍā** garam ho.
9. ṭhīk hai, yahāṁ ruko, ma͡ī abhī banātā hūṁ.

DAY 33: FOOD I

1. Would you like **tea** or **coffee**?
2. **Tea is good. I don't drink beer**.
3. Will you eat **meat** or **vegetables**?
4. I prefer **vegetables** and **fruits**.
5. **Bread or rice**?
6. **Bread** is good if it's warm.
7. How about **pasta** and **eggs**?
8. Yes, let the **pasta** be soft and the **egg** warm.
9. Alright, stay here, I'll make it now.

✤ India's national dish, Tandoori Chicken, was actually created by accident in the 1940s when a chef marinated chicken overnight in yogurt and spices and then cooked it in a tandoor.

दिन 34: खाद्य पदार्थ II

1. आज तुमने क्या खाया?
2. मैंने **सूप** और **सलाद** खाया।
3. **सूप** में क्या था?
4. **सूप** में **मक्खन, काली मिर्च और सब्ज़ियां** थीं।
5. और **सलाद** में?
6. **सलाद** में **पनीर और टमाटर** थे।
7. तुमने **सैंडविच** नहीं खाया?
8. नहीं, मैंने **सैंडविच** नहीं खाया।
9. चलो, फिर **चाय** पीते हैं।
10. हाँ, चलो।

✤ In Hindi, to express circumstances like time, place, or manner related to an action, especially when talking about foods, we use postpositions after the noun, like "में" (in), "के साथ" (with), and "से" (from).

1. āja tumane kyā khāyā?
2. maine **sūpa** aura **salāda** khāyā.
3. **sūpa** mẽ kyā thā?
4. **sūpa** mẽ **makkhana, kālī mirca aura sabzīyā̃** thī̃.
5. aura **salāda** mẽ?
6. **salāda** mẽ **panīra aura ṭamāṭara** the.
7. tumane **saiṇḍavica** nahī̃ khāyā?
8. nahī̃, maine **saiṇḍavica** nahī̃ khāyā.
9. calo, phira **cāya** pīte haiṃ.
10. hā̃, calo.

DAY 34: FOODS II

1. What did you eat today?
2. I ate **soup** and **salad**.
3. What was in the **soup**?
4. The **soup** had **butter, black pepper, and vegetables**.
5. And in the **salad**?
6. The **salad** had **cheese** and **tomatoes**.
7. Didn't you eat a **sandwich**?
8. No, I didn't eat a **sandwich**.
9. Let's have some **tea** then.
10. Yes, let's.

✣ Many traditional Indian recipes include spices not just for flavor, but also for their healing properties, as per Ayurveda.

दिन 35: पेय पदार्थ और मिठाइयाँ

1. आज तुम क्या पीना चाहोगे?
2. मुझे एक गिलास **पानी** और **जूस** चाहिए।
3. और खाने में?
4. मैं **चॉकलेट पाई** खाऊंगा।
5. मुझे **आइसक्रीम** और **टोस्ट** पसंद हैं।
6. **टोस्ट** पर क्या लगाओगे?
7. मक्खन और जाम।
8. अच्छा, मैं भी वही लूंगा।
9. ठीक है, मैं अभी ऑर्डर करता हूँ।

✣ In Hindi, an independent clause can stand alone as a sentence, like "मैं चाय पीता हूँ" (I drink tea), expressing a complete thought about drinks or desserts.

1. āja tuma kyā pīnā cāhoge?
2. mujhe eka gilāsa **pānī** aura **jūsa** cāhiye.
3. aura khāne meṃ?
4. maiṃ **cŏkaleṭa pā'ī** khā'ūṅgā.
5. mujhe **ā'iskrīma** aura **ṭōsṭa** pasanda haiṁ.
6. **ṭōsṭa** para kyā lagāoge?
7. makhaṇa aura jāma.
8. acchā, maiṃ bhī vahī lūṅgā.
9. ṭhīka hai, maiṃ abhī orḍara karatā hūṁ.

DAY 35: DRINKS AND DESSERTS

1. What would you like to drink today?
2. I would like a glass of **water** and **juice**.
3. And for food?
4. I'll have a **chocolate pie**.
5. I like **ice cream** and **toast**.
6. What will you put on the **toast**?
7. Butter and jam.
8. Okay, I'll have the same then.
9. Alright, I'll place the order now.

✤ The beloved Indian dessert Gulab Jamun was accidentally created by the personal chef of Mughal Emperor Shah Jahan, inspired to replicate the sweetness of his love for his wife, Mumtaz Mahal, for whom the Taj Mahal was also built.

दिन 36: खाना पकाने और रसोई

1. आज रात के खाने में क्या बना रहे हो?
2. **ग्रिल्ड** मांस और **भुनी हुई** सब्जियां बनाऊंगा।
3. ओह, अच्छा! क्या तुम **ओवन** का इस्तेमाल करोगे?
4. हां, और **फ्रिज** से ताजा सब्जियां निकालूंगा।
5. मैं मदद करूं? **प्लेटें** लगा दूं?
6. हां, और **कांटे**, **चम्मच, चाकू** भी रख दो।
7. ठीक है। पीने के लिए क्या लाऊं, **दूध** या **जूस**?
8. **जूस** अच्छा रहेगा। **बीयर** और **वाइन** भी है।
9. चलो, **जूस** और **वाइन** लेते हैं। शुक्रवार है, मनाते हैं!

✣ In Hindi, a subordinate clause, which gives extra information about the main action, often starts with "कि" (ki) when explaining a reason or detail related to cooking or kitchen activities.

1. āja rāta ke khāne mẽ kyā banā rahe ho?
2. **grilḍ** māṃsa aura **bhunī huī** sabzīyā̃ banāūṃgā.
3. Oha, acchā! kyā tuma **ovan** kā istemāla karoge?
4. hā̃, aura **phrij** se tājā sabzīyā̃ nikālūṃgā.
5. maiṃ madada karū̃? **pleṭeṃ** lagā dū̃?
6. hā̃, aura **kāṃṭe, cammacon, cāknū** bhī rakha do.
7. ṭhīka hai. pīne ke lie kyā lāū̃, **dūdha** yā **jūsa**?
8. **jūsa** acchā rahegā. **bīyara** aura **vāina** bhī hai.
9. calo, **jūsa** aura **vāina** lete haiṃ. śukravāra hai, manāte haiṃ!

1. What are you making for dinner tonight?
2. I'll make **grilled** meat and **roasted** vegetables.
3. Oh, nice! Will you use the **oven**?
4. Yes, and I'll take out fresh vegetables from the **fridge**.
5. Can I help? Should I set the **plates**?
6. Yes, and also put out the **forks, spoons, knives**.
7. Alright. What should I bring to drink, **milk** or **juice**?
8. **Juice would be good. There's also beer and wine.**
9. Let's go with **juice** and **wine**. It's Friday, let's celebrate!

✤ Sanjeev Kapoor, a celebrated Indian chef, popularized Indian cuisine globally through his show "Khana Khazana," making it the longest-running cookery show in Asia.

दिन 37: यात्रा और स्थान II

1. **समुद्र तट** पर चलोगे?
2. हां, **पहाड़** और **जंगल** देखना अच्छा लगेगा।
3. **नदी** के किनारे पिकनिक हो तो मजा आएगा।
4. **समुद्र** की लहरें और **महासागर** की गहराई कितनी सुंदर हैं!
5. **द्वीप** पर जाना है क्या?
6. नहीं, **घाटी** में ट्रेकिंग करेंगे।
7. **रेगिस्तान** में ऊंट की सवारी कैसी रहेगी?
8. अच्छा विचार है, पर **जंगल** सफारी भी तो है।
9. हां, वह भी करेंगे।

✣ In Hindi, to form a complex sentence about travel and places, you can combine two simple sentences using conjunctions like "क्योंकि" (because), "लेकिन" (but), or "अगर" (if), to show cause, contrast, or condition.

1. **samudra taṭ** para calogē?
2. hāṁ, **pahāṛ** aura **jaṅgala** dēkhanā accā lagēgā.
3. **nadī** kē kinārē piknika hō tō majā ā'ēgā.
4. **samudra** kī laharēṁ aura **mahāsāgara** kī gaharā'ī kitanī sundara haṁ!
5. **dvīpa** para jānā hai kyā?
6. nahīṁ, **ghāṭī** mēṁ ṭrēkiṅga karēṅgē.
7. **rēgistāna** mēṁ ūṁṭa kī savārī kaisī rahēgī?
8. accā vicāra hai, para **jaṅgala** saphārī bhī tō hai.
9. hāṁ, vaha bhī karēṅgē.

1. **Beach** walk, anyone?
2. Yes, seeing the **mountains** and **forests** would be nice.
3. A picnic by the **river** would be fun.
4. How beautiful are the waves of the **sea** and the depths of the **ocean**!
5. Want to go to an **island**?
6. No, we'll go trekking in the **valley**.
7. How about a camel ride in the **desert**?
8. Good idea, but there's also a **jungle** safari.
9. Yes, we'll do that too.

✤ Xuanzang, a Chinese Buddhist monk, traveled to India in the 7th century to gather sacred texts, significantly influencing the cultural exchange between India and China.

दिन 38: आपातकाल और स्वास्थ्य

1. आपको क्या हुआ?
2. मुझे **चोट** लग गई है और **एलर्जी** भी हो रही है।
3. तुम्हें **अस्पताल** जाना चाहिए। **डॉक्टर** को दिखाओ।
4. हाँ, मुझे **सहायता** की जरूरत है। क्या तुम **पुलिस** को फोन कर सकते हो?
5. मैं अभी करता हूँ। तुम **दवा** ले रहे हो?
6. हाँ, मैंने **गोली** ली है।
7. ठीक है, मैं **आग** के बारे में भी बता दूंगा।
8. शुक्रिया, मैं अब **आराम से** महसूस कर रहा हूँ।
9. अच्छा है। जल्दी स्वस्थ हो जाओ।

✤ In Hindi, the verb and adjectives in a sentence must agree in gender with the subject, so for emergencies and health, use "वह बीमार है" for 'he is sick' and "वह बीमार है" for 'she is sick', noting the verb doesn't change here but it does in other contexts.

1. āpko kyā hu'ā?
2. mujhe **coṭ** lag ga'ī hai aur **elarjī** bhī ho rahī hai.
3. tumheṃ **aspatāl** jānā cāhie. **ḍākṭar** ko dikhāo.
4. hām̐, mujhe **sahāyatā** kī jarūrat hai. kyā tum **pulis** ko phon kar sakte ho?
5. maiṃ abhī kartā hūm̐. tum **davā** le rahe ho?
6. hām̐, maine **golī** lī hai.
7. ṭhīk hai, maiṃ **āg** ke bāre meṃ bhī batā dūm̐gā.
8. śukriyā, maiṃ ab **ārām se** mahasūs kar rahā hūm̐.
9. acchā hai. jaldī svasth ho jāo.

1. What happened to you?
2. I've got a **wound** and I'm also having an **allergy**.
3. You should go to the **hospital**. See a **doctor**.
4. Yes, I need **help**. Can you call the **police**?
5. I'll do it right now. Are you taking any **medicine**?
6. Yes, I've taken a **pill**.
7. Okay, I'll also mention the **fire**.
8. Thank you, I'm feeling **comfortable** now.
9. That's good. Get well soon.

✣ In India, the ancient health system of Ayurveda, dating back over 3,000 years, emphasizes balance and wellness through natural remedies and practices.

1. **इक्कीस** लोग अस्पताल में हैं।
2. **बाईस** लोग पुलिस स्टेशन में हैं।
3. **तेईस** लोग आग से डरे हुए हैं।
4. **चौबीस** घंटे डॉक्टर सहायता करते हैं।
5. **पच्चीस** बच्चे स्कूल में भ्रमित हैं।
6. **छब्बीस** लोग ओवन के पास खड़े हैं।
7. **सत्ताईस** लोग फ्रिज देख रहे हैं।
8. **अट्ठाईस** प्लेटें मेज पर हैं।
9. **उनतीस** कांटे और चम्मच गिने गए?

❖ In Hindi, verbs and adjectives must agree in number with the nouns they describe or relate to, even when counting objects from 21 to 30.

1. **Ikkīsa** log aspatāl mem haĩ.
2. **Bāīsa** log pulis ṣṭeśan mem haĩ.
3. **Teīsa** log āg se ḍare hue haĩ.
4. **Caubīsa** ghaṇṭe ḍākṭar sahāyatā karte haĩ.
5. **Paccīsa** bacce skūl mem bhramit haĩ.
6. **Chabbīsa** log ovan ke pās khaṛe haĩ.
7. **Sattāīsa** log frij dekh rahe haĩ.
8. **Aṭṭhāīsa** pleṭem mej par haĩ.
9. **Unatīsa** kāṇṭe aur cammac giṇe gae?

DAY 39: NUMBERS 21-30

1. **Twenty-one** people are in the hospital.
2. **Twenty-two** people are in the police station.
3. **Twenty-three** people are scared of the fire.
4. **Twenty-four** hours doctors assist.
5. **Twenty-five** children are confused in school.
6. **Twenty-six** people are standing near the oven.
7. **Twenty-seven** people are looking at the fridge.
8. **Twenty-eight** plates are on the table.
9. **Twenty-nine** forks and spoons were counted?

✣ In ancient India, people played a game called "Jua" using nuts from the Vibhitaka tree as dice, which can be considered an early form of number games.

दिन 40: सप्ताह के दिन

1. **आज** शुक्रवार है। **कल** क्या तारीख होगी?
2. **कल** पच्चीस तारीख होगी। **कल शनिवार** होगा।
3. अच्छा, **कल** हम कहाँ जाएंगे?
4. **कल** हम समुद्र तट पर जाएंगे।
5. वहाँ कितने बजे?
6. दोपहर के बारह बजे।
7. मुझे समुद्र तट पर तैरना अच्छा लगता है।
8. हाँ, और मुझे रेत पर चलना पसंद है।
9. ठीक है, **कल** मिलते हैं।

✤ In Hindi, to compare days of the week, we often use "से" (se) for "than", as in "सोमवार को मंगलवार से ज्यादा पसंद है।" (Monday is liked more than Tuesday).

1. **āja** śukravāra hai. **kala** kyā tārīkha hogī?
2. **kala** paccīsa tārīkha hogī. **kala śanivāra** hogā.
3. acchā, **kala** hama kahām̐ jāem̐ge?
4. **kala** hama samudra taṭa para jāem̐ge.
5. vahām̐ kitane baje?
6. dopahara ke bāraha baje.
7. mujhe samudra taṭa para tairanā acchā lagatā hai.
8. hām̐, aura mujhe reta para calanā pasanda hai.
9. ṭhīka hai, **kala** milate haim̐.

1. **Today** is Friday. **Tomorrow** what date will it be?
2. **Tomorrow** will be the twenty-fifth. **Tomorrow** will be **Saturday**.
3. Okay, where will we go **tomorrow**?
4. **Tomorrow** we will go to the beach.
5. What time there?
6. At twelve in the afternoon.
7. I like swimming at the beach.
8. Yes, and I like walking on the sand.
9. Alright, see you **tomorrow**.

✤ In Hindu mythology, each day of the week is dedicated to a specific god, making certain days auspicious for specific activities.

CHALLENGE NO. 4

WRITE A LETTER OR EMAIL IN HINDI TO A FICTIONAL OR REAL FRIEND.

"स्वयं को बेहतर बनाने में लगे रहो।"

"Keep improving yourself."

दिन 41: सफाई I

1. सोमवार को मैंने **सोफ़ा** और **मेज़** साफ किया।
2. मंगलवार को **कुर्सी** और **बिस्तर** साफ किए।
3. बुधवार को **बाथरूम** की सफाई की।
4. गुरुवार को **रसोई** में **लैंप** साफ किया।
5. शुक्रवार को **दरवाज़े**, **खिड़कियाँ और दीवारें** धोईं।
6. **बाजार** गया, **दुकान** से सफाई का सामान **खरीदा**।
7. कुछ चीजें **महंगी** थीं, पर कुछ **सस्ती** थीं।
8. **सहायता** के लिए दोस्त को बुलाया।
9. सब मिलकर सफाई की।

✤ In Hindi, to form the superlative degree of an adjective, you often add "सबसे" (sabse) before the adjective, meaning "the most".

1. somavāra ko mainne **sophā** aura **mez** sāpha kiyā.
2. maṅgalavāra ko **kursī** aura **bistar** sāpha kie.
3. budhavāra ko **bātharūm** kī saphā'ī kī.
4. guruavāra ko **rasoī** meṁ **laimp** sāpha kiyā.
5. śukravāra ko **daravāze**, **khiṛakiyām̐ aura dīvāreṁ** dho'īṁ.
6. **bājār** gayā, **dukān** se saphā'ī kā sāmān **kharīdā**.
7. kuch cīzeṁ **mahaṅgī** thīṁ, para kuch **sastī** thīṁ.
8. **sahāyatā** ke lie dost ko bulāyā.
9. sab milkar saphā'ī kī.

DAY 41: CLEANING I

1. On Monday, I cleaned the **sofa** and **table**.
2. On Tuesday, cleaned the **chair** and **bed**.
3. On Wednesday, cleaned the **bathroom**.
4. On Thursday, cleaned the **lamp** in the **kitchen**.
5. On Friday, washed the **doors, windows, and walls**.
6. Went to the **market**, bought cleaning supplies from the **store**.
7. Some things were **expensive**, but some were **cheap**.
8. Called a friend for **help**.
9. Together, we cleaned everything.

✣ In many Indian homes, the first act of cleaning involves sweeping the floor with a broom made from the sacred neem tree, believed to also cleanse the space of negative energies.

दिन 42: सफाई II

1. आज **दिन** 42 है, हमें **घर** की **सफाई** करनी चाहिए।
2. हाँ, हम **अपार्टमेंट** के **कमरे** और **बालकनी** साफ करेंगे।
3. **छत** पर भी बहुत धूल है।
4. और **बगीचे**? वहाँ पत्तियाँ बिखरी हुई हैं।
5. **गैराज** में भी सामान बिखरा है, उसे भी व्यवस्थित करना होगा।
6. **सीढ़ियों** के **फर्श** को भी पोंछना है।
7. ठीक है, मैं **सोफ़ा** और **मेज़** को साफ करता हूँ।
8. मैं **कुर्सियों** और **बिस्तर** की धूल हटा दूँगी।
9. और **बाथरूम** की सफाई मैं करूँगा।

✤ In Hindi, to compare two things, we often use "से" (se) for "than" and change the adjective according to the degree of comparison, like "अच्छा" (good), "अच्छा से अच्छा" (better), "सबसे अच्छा" (best).

1. āja **dina** 42 hai, hamẽ **ghara** kī **saphā'ī** karanī cāhiye.
2. hām̐, hama **apārṭamẽṭa** ke **kamare** aura **bālakanī** sāpha kareṅge.
3. **chata** para bhī bahuta dhūla hai.
4. aura **bagīce**? vahām̐ pattiyām̐ bikharī hu'ī haim̐.
5. **gairāja** mem̐ bhī sāmāna bikharā hai, use bhī vyavasthita karanā hogā.
6. **sīṛhiyom̐** ke **pharśa** ko bhī pom̐chnā hai.
7. ṭhīka hai, maiṁ **sophā** aura **mez** ko sāpha karatā hūm̐.
8. maiṁ **kursiyom̐** aura **bistara** kī dhūla haṭā dūm̐gī.
9. aura **bāthrūma** kī saphā'ī maiṁ karūm̐gā.

DAY 42: CLEANING II

1. Today is **day** 42, we should clean the **house**.
2. Yes, we will clean the **apartment**'s **rooms and balcony**.
3. There's a lot of dust on the **roof** too.
4. And the **garden**? There are leaves scattered there.
5. There's also stuff scattered in the **garage**, that needs to be organized.
6. The **stairs**' **floor** also needs to be mopped.
7. Alright, I'll clean the **sofa and table**.
8. I'll remove the dust from the **chairs and bed**.
9. And I'll clean the **bathroom**.

✤ In ancient India, the concept of the modern refrigerator was predated by the use of large earthen pots called 'Surahi' to keep water cool through natural evaporation.

दिन 43: दिशा और स्थान II

1. **बाएँ** देखो, वहाँ एक बगीचा है।
2. हाँ, और **दाएँ** में एक अपार्टमेंट है।
3. **ऊपर** छत पर क्या है?
4. वहाँ लोग **चाय** पी रहे हैं।
5. **नीचे** क्या है?
6. **अंदर** कमरे में **सब्जियां** हैं।
7. **यहाँ** से रेलवे स्टेशन कैसे जाएँ?
8. **पीछे** से बस पकड़ो या **बगल में** टैक्सी स्टैंड है।
9. अच्छा, **बीच** से जाना होगा।

✤ In Hindi, to indicate direction or location, place the noun (place) first, followed by the postposition (like के पास, में) and then the verb at the end.

1. **bā'eṁ** dekho, vahām̐ ek bagīcā hai.
2. hām̐, aur **dā'eṁ** meṁ ek aparṭameṁṭ hai.
3. **ūpar** chhat par kyā hai?
4. vahām̐ log **cāy** pī rahe haiṁ.
5. **nīce** kyā hai?
6. **andar** kamre meṁ **sabjīyām̐** haiṁ.
7. **yahām̐** se relve stheśan kaise jāem̐?
8. **pīche** se bas pakaṛo yā **bagal meṁ** ṭaiksī sṭaim̐ḍ hai.
9. acchā, **bīc** se jānā hogā.

DAY 43: DIRECTION AND LOCATION II

1. **Look to the left**, there's a garden.
2. Yes, and **to the right** there's an apartment.
3. **What's on the roof** above?
4. There, people are **drinking tea**.
5. **What's below?**
6. **Inside**, the room has **vegetables**.
7. **How do we get to the railway station from here?**
8. **Catch a bus from behind** or there's a taxi stand **next to it**.
9. Alright, we'll have to go **through the middle**.

✣ India's Great Trigonometrical Survey, started in 1802, led to the discovery of the world's highest mountain, Mount Everest, initially named Peak XV.

दिन 44: शॉपिंग III

1. **मॉल** में जाना है?
2. हां, **सुपरमार्केट** से कुछ सामान लेना है।
3. **किराना दुकान** में भी जाना है क्या?
4. नहीं, बस **सुपरमार्केट** से पनीर और मक्खन लेना है।
5. **टोकरी** ले लो, आसानी होगी।
6. **कैश काउंटर** पर लंबी लाइन होगी।
7. अगर **कीमत** ज्यादा हुई तो **रिफंड** मिलेगा?
8. हां, और **छूट** भी देख लेना, **सेल** हो सकती है।
9. **रसीद** जरूर रखना।

✣ In Hindi, unlike English, the subject usually comes before the verb, but in questions, the order can invert, placing the verb before the subject.

1. **mŏl** mẽ jānā hai?
2. hā̃, **suparmārkeṭ** se kuch samān lenā hai.
3. **kirānā dukān** mẽ bhī jānā hai kyā?
4. nahī̃, bas **suparmārkeṭ** se panīr aur makhan lenā hai.
5. **ṭokarī** le lo, āsānī hogī.
6. **kaiś kāuṇṭar** par lambī lāin hogī.
7. agar **kīmat** jyādā huī to **riphaṇḍ** milegā?
8. hā̃, aur **chūṭ** bhī dekh lenā, **sel** ho saktī hai.
9. **rasīd** zarūr rakhnā.

DAY 44: SHOPPING III

1. Want to go to the **mall**?
2. Yes, I need to pick up some items from the **supermarket**.
3. Do we need to go to the **grocery store** as well?
4. No, just need to get cheese and butter from the **supermarket**.
5. Take a **basket**, it will be easier.
6. There might be a long line at the **cash counter**.
7. If the **price** is too high, will I get a **refund**?
8. Yes, and also check for any **discounts**, there might be a **sale**.
9. Make sure to keep the **receipt**.

✣ In Hindi culture, it's considered auspicious to give gifts in odd numbers, especially the number 11, symbolizing extra luck and prosperity.

दिन 45: पैसे और भुगतान

1. क्या आपके पास **नकद** है?
2. हां, मेरे पास कुछ **सिक्के** और **नोट** हैं।
3. मुझे **एटीएम** से **मुद्रा** निकालनी होगी।
4. क्या आप **डेबिट कार्ड** से भुगतान करेंगे?
5. नहीं, मैं **क्रेडिट कार्ड** का इस्तेमाल करूंगा।
6. **विनिमय दर** क्या है आज?
7. मैंने सुना है कि यह अच्छी है।
8. अच्छा, मैं कुछ **खरीदना** चाहता हूँ।
9. मैं भी, मुझे **बेचना** है।

✤ In Hindi, when talking about money and payments, the amount usually comes before the currency, followed by the verb at the end of the sentence.

1. kyaā āpake pās **nakada** hai?
2. hāṁ, mere pās kucha **sikke** aura **noṭa** haiṁ.
3. mujhe **ēṭīēma** se **mudrā** nikālanī hogī.
4. kyā āp **ḍēbiṭa kārḍa** se bhugatāna kareṁge?
5. nahīṁ, main **kreḍiṭa kārḍa** kā istemāla karūṁgā.
6. **vinimaya dara** kyā hai āja?
7. mainne sunā hai ki yaha acchī hai.
8. acchā, main kucha **kharīdanā** cāhatā hūṁ.
9. main bhī, mujhe **becanā** hai.

DAY 45: MONEY AND PAYMENTS

1. Do you have **cash**?
2. Yes, I have some **coins** and **notes**.
3. I will need to withdraw **currency** from the **ATM**.
4. Will you pay with a **debit card**?
5. No, I will use a **credit card**.
6. What is the **exchange rate** today?
7. I've heard it's good.
8. Good, I want to **buy** something.
9. Me too, I need to **sell**.

✣ In ancient India, people used grains and cattle as the first forms of money before coins were introduced.

दिन 46: समय और प्रकृति

1. आज **जलवायु** कैसी है?
2. **मौसम का पूर्वानुमान** कहता है कि आज **नम** रहेगा।
3. क्या **गरज** के साथ **बिजली** भी होगी?
4. हां, और शायद **बूंदाबांदी** भी होगी।
5. **धूप** कब निकलेगी?
6. दोपहर बाद **बादल** छंटेंगे।
7. क्या **इंद्रधनुष** दिखेगा?
8. अगर **बूंदाबांदी** के बाद **धूप** निकले तो हो सकता है।
9. अच्छा, मुझे **हिमकण** देखने का इंतजार है।

✤ In Hindi, to describe weather or nature, adjectives change form based on the gender and number of the noun they describe.

1. Auj **jalavāyu** kaisī hai?
2. **Mausam kā pūrvānumān** kahatā hai ki āj **nam** rahegā.
3. Kyā **garaj** ke sāth **bijlī** bhī hogī?
4. Hāṁ, aur śāyad **būndābāndī** bhī hogī.
5. **Dhūp** kab nikalegī?
6. Dopahar bād **bādal** chaṁṭeṁge.
7. Kyā **indr̥dhanuṣ** dikhēgā?
8. Agar **būndābāndī** ke bād **dhūp** nikale to ho saktā hai.
9. Acchā, mujhe **himakaṇ** dekhne kā iṁtazār hai.

1. What's the **weather** like today?
2. The **weather forecast** says it will be **humid** today.
3. Will there be **thunder** and **lightning** too?
4. Yes, and there might be **drizzle** as well.
5. When will the **sun** come out?
6. The **clouds** will clear after noon.
7. Will there be a **rainbow**?
8. If the **sun** comes out after the **drizzle**, it's possible.
9. Okay, I'm looking forward to seeing **snowflakes**.

✤ In Hindu mythology, the sacred river Ganges is believed to have descended from heaven to earth through the locks of Lord Shiva's hair.

दिन 47: आपदाएँ और भूगोल

1. कल **आंधी** आई थी, है ना?
2. हां, और **चक्रवात** का भी खतरा था।
3. **बवंडर** भी देखा क्या?
4. नहीं, पर **भूकंप** महसूस हुआ।
5. **ज्वालामुखी** तो नहीं फटा?
6. नहीं, वह तो दूसरे **महाद्वीप** पर है।
7. **तालाब** के पास **घाटी** में **गुफा** देखी?
8. हां, वहां बहुत **शांत** और **ठंडा** था।
9. अच्छा, चलो फिर कभी **नाला** के पास जाएंगे।

✤ In Hindi, the pronunciation of geographical names and disaster-related terms often involves aspirated consonants, like the breathy sound in "Bhūkamp" (भूकम्प) for earthquake.

1. kal **āndhī** ā'ī thī, hai nā?
2. hāṁ, aura **cakravāt** kā bhī khatrā thā.
3. **bavaṇḍar** bhī dekhā kyā?
4. nahīṁ, para **bhūkaṁp** mahasūs hu'ā.
5. **jvālāmukhī** to nahīṁ phaṭā?
6. nahīṁ, vah to dūsare **mahādvīp** para hai.
7. **tālāb** ke pās **ghāṭī** meṁ **gufā** dekhī?
8. hāṁ, vahāṁ bahut **śānt** aura **ṭhaṇḍā** thā.
9. acchā, calo phir kabhī **nālā** ke pās jā'eṅge.

DAY 47: DISASTERS AND GEOGRAPHY

1. There was a **storm** yesterday, wasn't there?
2. Yes, and there was also a threat of a **cyclone**.
3. Did you see a **tornado** as well?
4. No, but I felt an **earthquake**.
5. The **volcano** didn't erupt, did it?
6. No, that's on another **continent**.
7. Did you see the **cave** in the **valley** near the **pond**?
8. Yes, it was very **peaceful** and **cool** there.
9. Alright, let's go near the **stream** sometime then.

✤ In ancient Indian texts, it is believed that the god Indra used his thunderbolt to strike down demons causing droughts, symbolizing the natural disaster of lightning storms.

दिन 48: रंग

1. आज का दिन कैसा है?
2. **लाल** और **नीले** रंग बहुत सुंदर लग रहे हैं।
3. हां, **हरे** और **पीले** भी अच्छे लगते हैं।
4. तुम्हें **काला** या **सफेद** पसंद है?
5. मुझे **गुलाबी** और **भूरे** ज्यादा पसंद हैं।
6. **धूसर** रंग भी ठीक है।
7. हां, और **सोने** का रंग तो बहुत खास होता है।
8. चलो, रंगों के बारे में बात करते हुए चित्र बनाएं।
9. अच्छा विचार है!

✤ In Hindi, the pronunciation of color names can change slightly depending on the gender of the noun they describe.

1. āja kā dina kaisā hai?
2. **lāla** aura **nīlē** raṅga bahuta sundara laga rahē hā͡ĩ.
3. hām̐, **harē** aura **pīlē** bhī acchē lagatē hā͡ĩ.
4. tumhēm̐ **kālā** yā **saphēda** pasanda hai?
5. mujhē **gulābī** aura **bhūrē** jyādā pasanda hā͡ĩ.
6. **dhūsara** raṅga bhī ṭhīka hai.
7. hām̐, aura **sonē** kā raṅga tō bahuta khāsa hōtā hai.
8. calō, raṅgōṁ kē bārē mēṁ bāta karatē huē citra baṇāēm̐.
9. acchā vicāra hai!

1. How's the day today?
2. **Red** and **blue** colors are looking very beautiful.
3. Yes, **green** and **yellow** also look good.
4. Do you prefer **black** or **white**?
5. I like **pink** and **brown** more.
6. **Gray** color is also fine.
7. Yes, and the color of **gold** is very special.
8. Let's make paintings while talking about colors.
9. Good idea!

✤ During Holi, the festival of colors, people in India also celebrate the triumph of good over evil by lighting bonfires, symbolizing the burning of the demoness Holika.

दिन 49: प्रौद्योगिकी I

1. **इंटरनेट** पर मौसम का पूर्वानुमान देखा?
2. हां, **स्मार्टफोन** पर देखा। आज बारिश होगी।
3. **कंप्यूटर** पर भी देख सकते हैं।
4. मेरा **लैपटॉप** खराब है।
5. **ईमेल** से भी जानकारी मिल सकती है।
6. **वाई-फाई** चालू करो, **डाउनलोड** करना है।
7. **सोशल मीडिया** पर भी अपडेट मिलेगा।
8. **एप्लिकेशन** से आसान होता है।
9. **ब्राउज़र** खोलो, चेक करते हैं।

✣ In Hindi, when talking about technology, stress often falls on the first syllable of the word, making it sound clearer and more pronounced.

1. **iṇṭaranēṭ** para mausama kā pūrvānumāna dēkhā?
2. hāṁ, **smārṭphōna** para dēkhā. āja bāriśa hōgī.
3. **kampyūṭara** para bhī dēkha sakatē haiṁ.
4. mērā **laiṭapaṭa** kharāba hai.
5. **īmēla** sē bhī jānakārī mila sakatī hai.
6. **vāī-phāī** cālū karō, **ḍāunalōḍa** karanā hai.
7. **sōśala mīḍiyā** para bhī apaḍēṭa milēgā.
8. **aplīkēśana** sē āsāna hōtā hai.
9. **brauzara** khōlō, cēka karatē haiṁ.

DAY 49: TECHNOLOGY I

1. Checked the weather forecast on the **internet**?
2. Yes, saw it on my **smartphone**. It's going to rain today.
3. You can also check on a **computer**.
4. My **laptop** is broken.
5. You can also get information through **email**.
6. Turn on the **Wi-Fi**, need to **download**.
7. Updates are also available on **social media**.
8. It's easier with an **application**.
9. Open the **browser**, let's check.

✤ India's first newspaper, "Hicky's Bengal Gazette," was launched in 1780, marking the beginning of Indian journalism.

दिन 50: प्रौद्योगिकी II

1. **टेलीविजन** पर क्या देख रहे हो?
2. **समाचार** चैनल है। **रिमोट कंट्रोल** दो, मैं **वॉल्यूम** कम कर दूंगा।
3. **पासवर्ड** याद है? **लैपटॉप** खोलना है।
4. हां, **उपयोगकर्ता नाम** और **पासवर्ड** मैंने लिख रखे हैं।
5. **प्रिंटर** से कुछ प्रिंट करना है क्या?
6. नहीं, बस **ईमेल** चेक करना है।
7. **स्क्रीन** पर कुछ दिख नहीं रहा।
8. **कैमरा** चालू करो, वीडियो कॉल है।
9. ठीक है, **इंटरनेट** भी तेज है आज।

✣ In Hindi, there is no concept of written accent marks; instead, stress is understood through context and pronunciation practice.

1. **ṭēlīvijana** para kyā dēkha rahē hō?
2. **samācāra** cainaḷa hai. **rimōṭa kanṭrōla** dō, maiṁ **vŏlyūma** kama kara dūṅgā.
3. **pāsavarḍa** yāda hai? **laiṭŏpa** kholanā hai.
4. hāṁ, **upayōgakartā nāma** aura **pāsavarḍa** mainnē likha rakhē haiṁ̆.
5. **prinṭara** sē kucha prinṭa karanā hai kyā?
6. nahīṁ, basa **īmēla** cēka karanā hai.
7. **skrīna** para kucha dikha nahīṁ rahā.
8. **kaimarā** cālū karō, vīḍiyō kŏla hai.
9. ṭhīka hai, **inṭaranēṭa** bhī tēja hai āja.

1. **Television** - What are you watching?
2. It's a **news** channel. Give me the **remote control**, I'll lower the **volume**.
3. Do you remember the **password**? I need to open the **laptop**.
4. Yes, I have written down the **username** and **password**.
5. Do you need to print something from the **printer**?
6. No, just need to check **emails**.
7. Nothing is showing on the **screen**.
8. Turn on the **camera**, it's a video call.
9. Alright, the **internet** is also fast today.

✤ In India, a wedding invitation went viral on social media, leading to over 15,000 unexpected guests attending the celebration.

CHALLENGE NO. 5

LISTEN TO A PODCAST IN HINDI AND SUMMARIZE IT, IN WRITING OR ORALLY.

"जिज्ञासा ज्ञान की कुंजी है।"

"Curiosity is the key to knowledge."

दिन 51: जानवर

1. आज **सर्दी** का मौसम है। **गाय** और **घोड़े** खेत में हैं।
2. हाँ, और **कुत्ता** भी वहाँ है। **बिल्ली** कहाँ है?
3. **बिल्ली सोफे** पर सो रही है।
4. और **पक्षी**?
5. **पक्षी पेड़ पर हैं। मछलियाँ** तालाब में हैं।
6. **मुर्गी** क्या कर रही है?
7. **मुर्गी** अंडे दे रही है। **चूहा** और **सूअर** कहाँ हैं?
8. **चूहा** बाथरूम में है और **सूअर** कीचड़ में है।

✤ In Hindi, to link a subject (like an animal) with its action or description, we use the verb "है" (is) for singular and "हैं" (are) for plural, as in "बिल्ली सोती है" (The cat sleeps) and "कुत्ते भौंकते हैं" (The dogs bark).

1. Aujourd'hui, **sardi** kā mausam hai. **Gāya** aur **ghoṛe** khet meṃ haiṃ.
2. Hām̐, aur **kuttā** bhī vahām̐ hai. **Billī** kahām̐ hai?
3. **Billī sofe** par so rahī hai.
4. Aur **pakṣī**?
5. **Pakṣī peṛ par haiṃ. Machhaliyām̐** tālāb meṃ haiṃ.
6. **Murgī** kyā kar rahī hai?
7. **Murgī** aṇḍe de rahī hai. **Cūhā** aur **sūar** kahām̐ haiṃ?
8. **Cūhā** bāthrūm meṃ hai aur **sūar** kīcaṛ meṃ hai.

1. Today is **winter** weather. **Cows** and **horses** are in the field.
2. Yes, and the **dog** is there too. Where is the **cat**?
3. The **cat** is sleeping on the **sofa**.
4. And the **birds**?
5. The **birds** are on the tree. **Fish** are in the pond.
6. What is the **chicken** doing?
7. The **chicken** is laying eggs. Where are the **rat** and **pig**?
8. The **rat** is in the bathroom, and the **pig** is in the mud.

✤ The Royal Bengal Tiger, India's national animal, symbolizes strength, agility, and grace, embodying the spirit of the nation.

दिन 52: पौधे और प्रकृति 🌱

1. आज **पौधे** लगाने का दिन है।
2. हाँ, मैंने अपने **बगीचे** में एक नया **पेड़** और कुछ **फूल** लगाए हैं।
3. **घास** की चादर देखकर मन **प्रसन्न** हो जाता है।
4. सच में, हरा **पत्ता** देखकर आराम मिलता है।
5. **वन** और **जंगल** कितने सुंदर होते हैं!
6. हाँ, **पहाड़** और **नदी** के किनारे भी।
7. **महासागर** की लहरें सुनना भी सुकून देता है।
8. चलो, फिर **घर** की **छत** पर और पौधे लगाते हैं।
9. बहुत अच्छा विचार है!

✤ In Hindi, when two vowels come together due to word formation, especially in the context of plants and nature, one of the vowels is often dropped to make pronunciation easier, like in 'Vriksh' (वृक्ष) for 'tree', where 'a' in 'Vriksha' is elided.

1. Aaj paudhe lagane ka din hai.
2. Haan, maine apne bagiche mein ek naya ped aur kuch phool lagaye hain.
3. Ghaas ki chaadar dekhkar man prasann ho jata hai.
4. Sach mein, hara patta dekhkar aaram milta hai.
5. Van aur jungle kitne sundar hote hain!
6. Haan, pahaad aur nadi ke kinare bhi.
7. Mahasagar ki lahren sunna bhi sukoon deta hai.
8. Chalo, phir ghar ki chhat par aur paudhe lagate hain.
9. Bahut accha vichar hai!

1. Today is the day to plant **plants**.
2. Yes, I have planted a new **tree** and some **flowers** in my **garden**.
3. Seeing the blanket of **grass** makes the heart **happy**.
4. Truly, seeing green **leaves** brings peace.
5. How beautiful **forests** and **jungles** are!
6. Yes, the sides of **mountains** and **rivers** too.
7. Listening to the waves of the **ocean** also brings comfort.
8. Let's go, then plant more plants on the **roof** of the **house**.
9. That's a great idea!

✤ In ancient India, the Neem tree was considered a 'village pharmacy' because every part of it was used to treat various ailments.

दिन 53: संख्याएँ 31-40

1. **इकतीस** पौधे यहाँ हैं।
2. **बत्तीस** पेड़ दाएँ हैं।
3. **तैंतीस** फूल ऊपर टेबल पर हैं।
4. **चौंतीस** घास नीचे है।
5. **पैंतीस** पत्ते बाएँ हैं।
6. रिमोट कंट्रोल कहाँ है?
7. **छत्तीस** चैनल पर समाचार हैं।
8. मैं तनावग्रस्त और भ्रमित हूँ।
9. चिंतित मत हो, **चालीस** पर अच्छा कार्यक्रम है।

✤ In Hindi, when counting from 31 to 40, the word for "thirty" (तीस) contracts to "ती" before adding the numbers 1 through 9, like "तीएक" for 31, but remains "तीस" for 30 and "चालीस" for 40.

1. **ikatīsa** paudhe yahām̐ haiṁ.
2. **battīsa** peṛ dāem̐ haiṁ.
3. **taintīsa** phūla ūpara ṭebala para haim̐.
4. **caum̐tīsa** ghāsa nīce hai.
5. **paintīsa** patte bāem̐ haim̐.
6. rimoṭa kam̐ṭrola kahām̐ hai?
7. **chaṭṭīsa** cainala para samācāra haim̐.
8. maiṁ tanāvagrasta aura bhramita hūm̐.
9. cintita mata ho, **cālīsa** para acchā kāryakrama hai.

DAY 53: NUMBERS 31-40

1. **Thirty-one** plants are here.
2. **Thirty-two** trees are on the right.
3. **Thirty-three** flowers are on the table above.
4. **Thirty-four** grass is below.
5. **Thirty-five** leaves are on the left.
6. Where is the remote control?
7. **Thirty-six** channels have news.
8. I am stressed and confused.
9. Don't worry, there is a good program on **forty**.

✤ India's Parliament House, a masterpiece of architecture, has 247 pillars, symbolizing the strength and unity of the country.

दिन 54: संगीत और मनोरंजन

1. **संगीत** सुनना अच्छा लगता है?
2. हां, मुझे **गाने** बहुत पसंद हैं।
3. तुम्हें कौन सा **गायक** या **गायिका** पसंद है?
4. मुझे एक **बैंड** बहुत अच्छा लगता है।
5. वे कौन से **वाद्ययंत्र** बजाते हैं?
6. वे **मंच** पर भी प्रदर्शन करते हैं।
7. क्या तुमने उनकी **फिल्म** देखी है?
8. नहीं, पर मैंने **रेडियो** पर सुना है।
9. **नृत्य** और **कॉन्सर्ट** में जाना पसंद है?

✤ In Hindi, determiners like "kuch" (some) and "sab" (all) are used before nouns to talk about quantities or amounts, as in "kuch gaane" (some songs) for today's theme of music and entertainment.

1. **saṅgīta** sunanā acchā lagatā hai?
2. hāṁ, mujhe **gāne** bahut pasand hain.
3. tumheṁ kaun sā **gāyaka** yā **gāyikā** pasand hai?
4. mujhe ek **baiṇḍa** bahut acchā lagatā hai.
5. ve kaun se **vādyayantra** bajāte hain?
6. ve **manca** para bhī pradarśana karate hain.
7. kyā tumne unakī **philm** dekhī hai?
8. nahīṁ, para maine **reḍiyō** para sunā hai.
9. **nṛtya** aura **kānsarṭa** meṁ jānā pasand hai?

1. Do you like listening to **music**?
2. Yes, I really like **songs**.
3. Which **singer** or **female singer** do you like?
4. I really like a **band**.
5. What **instruments** do they play?
6. They also perform on **stage**.
7. Have you seen their **movie**?
8. No, but I have heard them on the **radio**.
9. Do you like going to **dance** and **concerts**?

✣ The sitar, a plucked string instrument, became globally renowned thanks to Ravi Shankar's performances at Woodstock and the Monterey Pop Festival.

1. **हवाई अड्डा** पर **हवाई जहाज** कब आएगा?
2. **रेलगाड़ी** से जाना बेहतर है, **रेलवे स्टेशन** पास है।
3. **बस** या **कार** से कितना समय लगेगा?
4. **टैक्सी** तेज होगी, पर **साइकिल** से नहीं जा सकते।
5. **जहाज** से जाना है तो **बंदरगाह** जाना पड़ेगा।
6. **बस** टिकट के लिए **नकद** या **क्रेडिट कार्ड**?
7. **डेबिट कार्ड से भी चलेगा। एटीएम** कहाँ है?
8. **एटीएम रेलवे स्टेशन** के पास ही है।
9. चलो, फिर **बस** से चलते हैं।

✤ In Hindi, to express quantity or amount, place the quantifier after the noun, for example, "car do" means "two cars".

1. **havāī aḍḍā** par **havāī jahāj** kab ā'egā?
2. **relgāṛī** se jānā behtar hai, **relve stēśan** pās hai.
3. **bas** yā **kār** se kitanā samay lagegā?
4. **ṭaiksī** tej hogī, par **sa'ikal** se nahīṁ jā sakte.
5. **jahāj** se jānā hai to **bandargāh** jānā paṛegā.
6. **bas** ṭikaṭ ke lie **nakaḍ** yā **kreḍiṭ kārḍ**?
7. **ḍebiṭ kārḍ se bhī calegā. eṭīem** kahām̐ hai?
8. **eṭīem relve stēśan** ke pās hī hai.
9. calo, phir **bas** se calte haiṁ.

1. When will the **airplane** arrive at the **airport**?
2. It's better to go by **train**, the **railway station** is close.
3. How long will it take by **bus** or **car**?
4. A **taxi** will be faster, but you can't go by **bicycle**.
5. If you want to go by **ship**, you'll need to go to the **port**.
6. **Bus ticket** - **cash or credit card**?
7. **Debit card** will also work. Where is the **ATM**?
8. The **ATM** is near the **railway station**.
9. Let's go by **bus** then.

✣ India's Mars Orbiter Mission, Mangalyaan, was so cost-effective that it was cheaper than the Hollywood movie "Gravity."

दिन 56: शॉपिंग II

1. क्या तुम **मॉल** जाना चाहते हो?
2. हां, मुझे **कपड़े** और **जैकेट** खरीदने हैं।
3. **सुपरमार्केट** में भी चलेंगे?
4. ज़रूर, मुझे **किराने की दुकान** से सामान भी लेना है।
5. वहां **सेल** है, **छूट** मिलेगी।
6. अच्छा! मैं **आभूषण** भी देखूंगा।
7. **हार** और **झुमके** खरीदना है क्या?
8. हां, मेरी बहन के लिए।
9. चलो फिर, जल्दी चलते हैं।

✤ In Hindi, to show possession, add "का" (ka), "की" (ki), or "के" (ke) after the possessor noun depending on the gender and number of the object possessed.

1. kyā tum **mŏl** jānā cāhte ho?
2. hām̐, mujhe **kapaṛe** aur **jaiket** kharīdne haim̐.
3. **suparmārkeṭ** mem̐ bhī caleṅge?
4. zarūr, mujhe **kirāne kī dukān** se sāmān bhī lenā hai.
5. vahām̐ **sel** hai, **chūṭ** milegī.
6. acchā! main **ābhūṣaṇ** bhī dekhūṅgā.
7. **hār** aur **jhumke** kharīdnā hai kyā?
8. hām̐, merī bahan ke lie.
9. calo phir, jaldī calte haim̐.

DAY 56: SHOPPING II

1. Do you want to go to the **mall**?
2. Yes, I need to buy **clothes** and a **jacket**.
3. Shall we also go to the **supermarket**?
4. Sure, I also need to pick up some stuff from the **grocery store**.
5. There's a **sale** there, we'll get a **discount**.
6. Great! I'll also look at **jewelry**.
7. Do you want to buy a **necklace** and **earrings**?
8. Yes, for my sister.
9. Let's go then, let's hurry.

✣ In India, flea markets like Goa's Anjuna Market are vibrant cultural hubs where bargaining is an art form.

दिन 57: शरीर और स्वास्थ्य II

1. कल मैंने **जैकेट** खरीदी।
2. अच्छा? कहाँ से?
3. मॉल से। वहाँ **कपड़े** बहुत सुंदर थे।
4. तुमने **संगीत** की दुकान देखी?
5. हाँ, वहाँ एक **बैंड** बज रहा था।
6. **गायक** कैसा था?
7. बहुत अच्छा! मैंने एक **गाना** भी खरीदा।
8. फिर हम **चाय** पीने चलें?
9. हाँ, चलो। **कॉफ़ी** भी अच्छी होगी।

✤ In Hindi, to point out something close, use "यह" (this) for "near" and "वह" (that) for "far" when talking about body parts or health issues.

1. kal mainne **jaikēṭ** kharīdī.
2. acchā? kahām̐ se?
3. mŏl se. vahām̐ **kapaṛe** bahut sundar the.
4. tumne **sangīt** kī dukān dekhī?
5. hām̐, vahām̐ ek **baim̐ḍ** baj rahā thā.
6. **gāyak** kaisā thā?
7. bahut acchā! mainne ek **gānā** bhī kharīdā.
8. phir ham **cāy** pīne calem̐?
9. hām̐, calo. **kŏphī** bhī acchī hogī.

1. Yesterday, I bought a **jacket**.
2. Oh? Where from?
3. From the mall. The **clothes** there were very beautiful.
4. Did you see the **music** store?
5. Yes, there was a **band** playing.
6. How was the **singer**?
7. Very good! I also bought a **song**.
8. Shall we go for some **tea** then?
9. Yes, let's go. **Coffee** would be nice too.

✤ In traditional Indian medicine, Ayurveda, it's believed that chewing on neem leaves can purify the blood and support immune health.

दिन 58: व्यवसाय और काम I

1. आज हम रंगों के बारे में सीखेंगे। यह क्या रंग है?
2. यह लाल है।
3. बहुत अच्छा! और यह?
4. यह हरा है।
5. अब, तुम वकील बनो और मुझसे पूछो।
6. आपकी कार का रंग क्या है?
7. मेरी कार नीली है। और तुम्हारी?
8. मेरी कार काली है।
9. शाबाश! अब हम खाने की चीजों के बारे में सीखेंगे।
10. मुझे पनीर पसंद है।

✤ In Hindi, to describe someone's profession, we use the structure "X Y हैं," where X is the person and Y is the profession, with "का," "की," or "के" added between X and Y if needed to show relation.

1. āja hama raṅgoṁ ke bāre meṁ sīkheṅge. yaha kyā raṅga hai?
2. yaha lāla hai.
3. bahuta acchā! aura yaha?
4. yaha harā hai.
5. aba, tuma vakīla bano aura mujhase pūcho.
6. āpakī cāra kā raṅga kyā hai?
7. merī cāra nīlī hai. aura tumhārī?
8. merī cāra kālī hai.
9. śābāśa! aba hama khāne kī cīzoṁ ke bāre meṁ sīkheṅge.
10. mujhe panīra pasanda hai.

1. Today we will learn about colors. What color is this?
2. This is red.
3. Very good! And this?
4. This is green.
5. Now, you be the lawyer and ask me.
6. What color is your car?
7. My car is blue. And yours?
8. My car is black.
9. Well done! Now we will learn about food items.
10. I like cheese.

✤ In India, the art of creating vibrant Madhubani paintings, a tradition over 2,500 years old, was originally practiced by women on the walls and floors of their homes.

दिन 59: घरेलू सामान II

1. क्या तुमने **फ्रिज** में **दूध** रखा?
2. हां, और मैंने **ओवन** में केक भी बेक किया है।
3. **मेज** पर **घड़ी** कहाँ है?
4. वह **खिड़की** के पास **लैंप** के बगल में है।
5. क्या **दरवाजा** बंद है?
6. नहीं, मैं अभी बंद करता हूँ।
7. **सोफा** पर **कुर्सी** क्यों है?
8. अरे, वह तो मैंने सफाई के लिए रखी थी।
9. ठीक है, अब मैं **बिस्तर** पर आराम करूँगा।

✣ In Hindi, to talk about indefinite household items, we often use "kuch" (कुछ) before the noun, like "kuch kitaaben" (कुछ किताबें) meaning "some books".

1. kya tumne **phrij** meṃ **dūdh** rakhā?
2. hām̐, aur mainne **ovan** meṃ kek bhī bek kiyā hai.
3. **mez** par **ghaṛī** kahām̐ hai?
4. vah **khiṛkī** ke pās **laimp** ke bagal meṃ hai.
5. kyā **daravājā** bam̐d hai?
6. nahīm̐, main abhī bam̐d karatā hūm̐.
7. **sophā** par **kursī** kyoṃ hai?
8. are, vah to mainne saphāī ke lie rakhī thī.
9. ṭhīk hai, ab main **bistar** par ārām karūm̐gā.

DAY 59: HOUSEHOLD ITEMS II

1. Did you put the **milk** in the **fridge**?
2. Yes, and I also baked a cake in the **oven**.
3. Where is the **clock** on the **table**?
4. It's next to the **lamp** near the **window**.
5. Is the **door** closed?
6. No, I'll close it now.
7. Why is there a **chair** on the **sofa**?
8. Oh, I had placed it there for cleaning.
9. Alright, now I'm going to rest on the **bed**.

✣ India invented the game of chess, originally called "Chaturanga," over 1,500 years ago.

दिन 60: माप और आकार

1. **आकार** क्या है इस सोफे का?
2. **लंबाई** दो **मीटर** है और **चौड़ाई** एक **मीटर**।
3. **ऊंचाई** कितनी है?
4. यह साठ **सेंटीमीटर** है।
5. और **वजन**?
6. लगभग पचास **किलोग्राम**।
7. फ्रिज का **आकार**?
8. ऊंचाई एक सौ बीस **सेंटीमीटर**, **चौड़ाई** सत्तर **सेंटीमीटर**।
9. और **शेप**?
10. वर्गाकार।

✤ In Hindi, to form the present participle of verbs related to measurements and size, add "ते हुए" (te hue) to the root verb, indicating an ongoing action, like "नापते हुए" (napte hue) for "measuring."

1. **ākāra** kyā hai is sofe kā?
2. **lambā'ī** do **mīṭara** hai aura **cauṛā'ī** eka **mīṭara**.
3. **ũcā'ī** kitanī hai?
4. yaha sāṭha **senṭīmīṭara** hai.
5. aura **vajana**?
6. lagabhaga pacāsa **kilōgrāma**.
7. phrij kā **ākāra**?
8. ũcā'ī eka sau bīsa **senṭīmīṭara**, **cauṛā'ī** sattara **senṭīmīṭara**.
9. aura **śēpa**?
10. vargākāra.

DAY 60: MEASUREMENTS AND SIZE

1. **What is the size** of this sofa?
2. **The length** is two **meters** and **the width** is one **meter**.
3. **How tall** is it?
4. It is sixty **centimeters** tall.
5. And **the weight**?
6. About fifty **kilograms**.
7. **What's the size** of the fridge?
8. **The height** is one hundred twenty **centimeters**, **the width** seventy **centimeters**.
9. And **the shape**?
10. Square.

✤ Ancient India had a sophisticated measurement system called "Vastu Shastra," used for architecture and city planning, aligning buildings with the cosmic order.

CHALLENGE NO. 6

RECORD A SHORT AUDIO WHERE YOU TALK ABOUT YOUR PROGRESS IN HINDI.

"संस्कृतियों का सम्मान करना सीखो, क्योंकि विविधता में एकता है।"

"Learn to respect cultures, for there is unity in diversity."

दिन 61: भोजन और पोषण II

1. क्या तुमने **पास्ता** खाया?
2. हां, मैंने **मक्खन** और **काली मिर्च** के साथ खाया।
3. **चिकन** या **गाय का मांस**?
4. मैंने **चिकन** चुना।
5. **रोटी** या **चावल**?
6. **रोटी** के साथ।
7. और **पनीर**?
8. बिल्कुल, वह बहुत स्वादिष्ट था।
9. मिठाई में क्या लिया?
10. **आइसक्रीम**!

✤ In Hindi, to form the past participle of a verb related to food, like "cooked" (पकाया), add "या" to the root verb "to cook" (पका).

1. kyā tumne **pāstā** khāyā?
2. hām̐, mainne **makhan** aur **kālī mirca** ke sāth khāyā.
3. **cikan** yā **gāy kā māṃs**?
4. mainne **cikan** cunā.
5. **roṭī** yā **cāval**?
6. **roṭī** ke sāth.
7. aur **panīr**?
8. bilkuṭ, vah bahut svādiṣṭ thā.
9. miṭhāī meṃ kyā liyā?
10. **āiskrīm**!

DAY 61: FOOD AND NUTRITION II

1. Did you eat **pasta**?
2. Yes, I ate it with **butter** and **black pepper**.
3. **Chicken or beef**?
4. I chose **chicken**.
5. **Bread or rice**?
6. With **bread**.
7. And **cheese**?
8. Absolutely, it was very delicious.
9. What did you have for dessert?
10. **Ice cream**!

✤ India introduced the world to the art of seasoning with spices, revolutionizing global cuisine.

दिन 62: सप्ताह के दिन

1. **सोमवार** को मैंने पास्ता बनाया।
2. **मंगलवार** को मैंने मक्खन और काली मिर्च डाली।
3. **बुधवार** को गाय का मांस खरीदा।
4. **गुरुवार** को चिकन पकाया।
5. **शुक्रवार** को सोफे पर आराम किया।
6. **शनिवार** को ओवन साफ किया।
7. **रविवार** को फ्रिज में कुछ नहीं था।
8. **सप्ताहांत** में मैंने पौधे लगाए।
9. **कल** मुझे डॉक्टर की सहायता चाहिए थी।

✤ In Hindi, to form a gerund (continuous action) related to days of the week, add "कर" to the day's name, like "सोमवार कर" for "doing Monday" (meaning engaging in Monday's activities).

1. **Somavāra** ko mainne pāstā banāyā.
2. **Maṅgalavāra** ko mainne makẖana aura kālī mirca ḍālī.
3. **Budhavāra** ko gāya kā māṃsa kharīdā.
4. **Guruvāra** ko cikana pakāyā.
5. **Śukravāra** ko sofe para ārāma kiyā.
6. **Śanivāra** ko ovan sāpha kiyā.
7. **Ravivāra** ko frija meṃ kucha nahīṃ thā.
8. **Saptāhānta** meṃ mainne paudhe lagāe.
9. **Kala** mujhe ḍākṭar kī sahāyatā cāhie thī.

DAY 62: DAYS OF THE WEEK

1. **Monday**, I made pasta.
2. **Tuesday**, I added butter and black pepper.
3. **Wednesday**, I bought beef.
4. **Thursday**, I cooked chicken.
5. **Friday**, I relaxed on the sofa.
6. **Saturday**, I cleaned the oven.
7. **Sunday**, there was nothing in the fridge.
8. **Over the weekend**, I planted some plants.
9. **Yesterday**, I needed a doctor's help.

✤ In Hindi culture, it's considered auspicious to start new ventures on Wednesday, attributed to Mercury's influence, which governs growth and intellect.

दिन 63: मौसम और ऋतुएँ

1. **आज** सुबह मौसम कैसा है?
2. **कल** बहुत गर्मी थी।
3. **दिन** भर धूप रहेगी या बादल आएंगे?
4. **रात** को तो सर्दी बढ़ जाती है।
5. **दोपहर** में वसंत की हवा अच्छी लगती है।
6. **शाम** को पतझड़ के पत्ते गिरते हैं।
7. हां, और **वसंत** में फूल खिलते हैं।
8. **सर्दी** में तो बस रजाई में रहने का मन करता है।
9. हां, मौसम बदलता रहता है।

✤ In Hindi, to express wanting to do something related to weather or seasons, use the infinitive form by adding "ना" to the verb, like "बारिश में भीगना" (wanting to get drenched in the rain).

1. **āja** subaha mausama kaisā hai?
2. **kala** bahuta garmī thī.
3. **dina** bhara dhūpa rahegī yā bādala āēṅgē?
4. **rāta** kō tō saradī baṛha jātī hai.
5. **dōpahara** mēṁ vasanta kī havā acchī lagatī hai.
6. **śāma** kō patajhaṛa kē pattē giratē haṁ.
7. hām̐, aura **vasanta** mēṁ phūla khilatē haṁ.
8. **sardī** mēṁ tō basa rajā'ī mēṁ rahanē kā mana karatā hai.
9. hām̐, mausama badalatā rahatā hai.

1. **Today** morning, how's the weather?
2. **Yesterday** it was very hot.
3. Will it be sunny all **day** or will clouds come?
4. At **night**, it gets colder.
5. In the **afternoon**, the spring breeze feels nice.
6. In the **evening**, the autumn leaves fall.
7. Yes, and in **spring**, flowers bloom.
8. In **winter**, you just feel like staying in a quilt.
9. Yes, the weather keeps changing.

✤ In India, the monsoon season is celebrated through numerous songs, capturing the rejuvenating essence of rain and its romantic allure in Bollywood films.

दिन 64: परिवार II

1. **चाची**, आज शाम को आप क्या बना रही हैं?
2. बेटा, मैं पास्ता बना रही हूँ, उसमें मक्खन और काली मिर्च डालूँगी।
3. **मौसी**, क्या मैं आपकी मदद कर सकता हूँ?
4. हाँ **भतीजे**, तुम मक्खन निकाल दो।
5. **बुआ**, कल रात को आपके **सहकर्मी** का बैंड बहुत अच्छा बजा था।
6. हाँ **पोती**, उनके गाने भी बहुत सुंदर थे।
7. **ताई**, आपकी **चचेरी बहन** कब आएँगी?
8. वह गुरुवार को आएँगी, **भतीजी**।
9. ठीक है, मैं उनके लिए चिकन बनाऊँगी।

✣ In Hindi, many family-related words can be formed by adding suffixes to the root word "परिवार" (parivaar), which means family.

1. **cācī**, āja śāma ko āpa kyā banā rahī haiṁ?
2. beṭā, maiṁ pāstā banā rahī hūm̐, usmeṁ makkhana aura kālī mirca ḍālūm̐gī.
3. **mausī**, kyā maiṁ āpakī madada kara saktā hūm̐?
4. hām̐ **bhatīje**, tuma makkhana nikāla do.
5. **bu'ā**, kala rāta ko āpake **sahakarmī** kā baiṁḍa bahuta acchā bajā thā.
6. hām̐ **potī**, unake gāne bhī bahuta sundara the.
7. **tā'ī**, āpakī **cacarī bahana** kaba āyem̐gī?
8. vaha guruvara ko āyem̐gī, **bhatījī**.
9. ṭhīka hai, maiṁ unake lie cikana banāūm̐gī.

DAY 64: FAMILY II

1. **Auntie**, what are you making this evening?
2. Child, I'm making pasta, I'll add butter and black pepper to it.
3. **Aunt**, can I help you with anything?
4. Yes **nephew**, please take out the butter.
5. **Aunt**, your **colleague's** band played really well last night.
6. Yes **granddaughter**, their songs were also very beautiful.
7. **Aunt**, when will your **cousin sister** arrive?
8. She will come on Thursday, **niece**.
9. Alright, I'll make chicken for her.

✣ In traditional Indian families, stories of ancestors are often passed down as a way to teach moral values and preserve history.

दिन 65: दिशाएँ और स्थान III

1. **बाएँ** मुड़ें, फिर **सीधे** जाएँ।
2. **दाएँ** देखिए, वहाँ एक **सोफ़ा** और **मेज़** है।
3. **ऊपर** के कमरे में **बिस्तर** के **पास** एक **कुर्सी** है।
4. **नीचे** क्या है?
5. वहाँ एक **बाथरूम** है।
6. **रुकें**, यह **दूर** नहीं है।
7. हाँ, यह तो **बीच** में है।
8. अच्छा, चलिए **पास** ही चलते हैं।
9. हाँ, चलिए।

✣ In Hindi, verbs change form based on the direction or location mentioned, for example, "jana" (to go) becomes "gaya" (went) when talking about going somewhere in the past.

1. **bā'eṁ** muḍeṁ, phir **sīdhe** jāeṁ।
2. **dā'eṁ** dekhiye, vahām̐ ek **sofā** aur **mez** hai।
3. **ūpar** ke kamre meṁ **bistar** ke **pās** ek **kursī** hai।
4. **nīce** kyā hai?
5. vahām̐ ek **bāthrūm** hai।
6. **rukeṁ**, yah **dūr** nahīṁ hai।
7. hām̐, yah to **bīc** meṁ hai।
8. acchā, caliye **pās** hī calte haiṁ।
9. hām̐, caliye।

DAY 65: DIRECTIONS AND LOCATIONS III

1. Turn **left**, then go **straight**.
2. Look to the **right**, there is a **sofa** and a **table**.
3. In the room **above**, there is a **chair** next to the **bed**.
4. What's **below**?
5. There is a **bathroom**.
6. **Stop, it's not far**.
7. Yes, it's right in the **middle**.
8. Alright, let's go **nearby**.
9. Yes, let's go.

✤ In the Indian epic "Ramayana," Lord Rama's 14-year exile is a transformative journey that shapes the essence of duty, love, and dharma.

दिन 66: भावनाएँ II

1. **उत्साहित** होकर, "मैं कल मॉल जाऊंगा।"
2. "मैं भी **गर्वित** हूँ, मेरा नया अपार्टमेंट देखो।"
3. "मैं **चिंतित** हूँ, क्या तुम मुझे सुपरमार्केट तक रास्ता बता सकते हो?"
4. "हाँ, सीधे जाओ फिर दाएँ मुड़ो।"
5. "मैं **घबराया हुआ** हूँ, अगर मैं रास्ता भूल गया तो?"
6. "चिंता मत करो, अगर तुम **भ्रमित** हो जाओ तो रुक जाना और पूछ लेना।"
7. "ठीक है, मैं **प्रसन्न** हूँ कि तुमने मदद की।"
8. "मैं **तनावग्रस्त** नहीं हूँ, अब मैं **आराम** से हूँ।"
9. "अच्छा है, शाम को बगीचे में **क्रोधित** न होना।"

✤ In Hindi, to express emotions in compound tenses, we combine the verb expressing the emotion with the appropriate form of "होना" (to be) to match the tense.

1. **utsāhita** hokar, "maiṁ kala mōla jāūṅgā."
2. "maiṁ bhī **garvita** hūm̐, mērā nayā aparṭamĕṁṭa dēkhō."
3. "maiṁ **cintita** hūm̐, kyā tuma mujhē suparamārkeṭa taka rāstā batā sakatē hō?"
4. "hām̐, sīdhē jā'ō phira dāēm̐ muḍō."
5. "maiṁ **ghabrayā hu'ā** hūm̐, agar maiṁ rāstā bhūla gayā tō?"
6. "cintā mata karō, agar tuma **bhramita** hō jā'ō tō ruka jānā aura pūcha lēnā."
7. "ṭhīka hai, maiṁ **prasanna** hūm̐ ki tumaṇē madada kī."
8. "maiṁ **tanāvagrasta** nahīm̐ hūm̐, aba maiṁ **ārāma** sē hūm̐."
9. "acchā hai, śāma kō bagīcē mēṁ **krōdhita** na hōnā."

1. **Excitedly**, "I will go to the mall tomorrow."
2. "I am also **proud**, look at my new apartment."
3. "I am **worried**, can you tell me the way to the supermarket?"
4. "Yes, go straight then turn right."
5. "I am **nervous**, what if I forget the way?"
6. "Don't worry, if you get **confused** just stop and ask."
7. "Okay, I am **happy** that you helped."
8. "I am not **stressed**, now I am **relaxed**."
9. "Good, don't be **angry** in the garden in the evening."

✤ In traditional Indian art, emotions are vividly depicted through the intricate facial expressions and hand gestures of classical dance forms.

दिन 67: प्रौद्योगिकी और मीडिया

1. क्या तुमने नया **स्मार्टफोन** खरीदा?
2. हाँ, मैंने **ऑनलाइन** एक अच्छी **वेबसाइट** से खरीदा।
3. उसमें **वाई-फाई** है?
4. हाँ, और मैं **ईमेल** भी चेक कर सकता हूँ।
5. तुम **सोशल मीडिया** पर हो?
6. हाँ, मैंने **एप्लिकेशन** डाउनलोड किए हैं।
7. और **ब्लॉग** पढ़ते हो?
8. कभी-कभी, मैं **ब्राउज़र** से पढ़ता हूँ।
9. बहुत अच्छा, **इंटरनेट** से ज्ञान बढ़ता है।

✤ In Hindi, to express the infinitive mood related to technology and media, add "ना" to the verb root, like "देखना" (to watch) or "सुनना" (to listen).

1. kyā tumne nayā **smārṭaphōna** kharīdā?
2. hām̐, mainne **onlāina** eka acchī **vebasāiṭa** se kharīdā.
3. usmeṃ **vāī-phāī** hai?
4. hām̐, aura main **īmela** bhī ceka kara saktā hūm̐.
5. tum **sośala mīḍiyā** para ho?
6. hām̐, mainne **eplikeśana** ḍāunalōḍa kie haim̐.
7. aura **blŏga** paṛhate ho?
8. kabhī-kabhī, main **brauzara** se paṛhatā hūm̐.
9. bahuta acchā, **inṭaraneṭa** se jñāna baṛhatā hai.

DAY 67: TECHNOLOGY AND MEDIA

1. Did you buy a new **smartphone**?
2. Yes, I bought it **online** from a good **website**.
3. Does it have **Wi-Fi**?
4. Yes, and I can also check **emails**.
5. Are you on **social media**?
6. Yes, I have downloaded **applications**.
7. And do you read **blogs**?
8. Sometimes, I read them through a **browser**.
9. Very good, **internet** increases knowledge.

✣ India's first newspaper, "Hicky's Bengal Gazette," was launched in 1780, marking the dawn of journalism in the country.

दिन 68: पढ़ाई और कला

1. **पाठ** के लिए तुम कौन सी **किताब** पढ़ रहे हो?
2. मैं एक **उपन्यास** पढ़ रहा हूँ, यह **काल्पनिक** है।
3. क्या तुम्हें **कविता** पढ़ना पसंद है?
4. हाँ, मुझे **कविताएँ** और **गैर-काल्पनिक** साहित्य दोनों पसंद हैं।
5. तुम **चित्रकला** या **फोटोग्राफी** में भी रुचि रखते हो?
6. मुझे **चित्र** बनाना और **गाना** बहुत पसंद है।
7. मैं भी, मैं इंटरनेट पर **ऑनलाइन चित्रकला** सीख रहा हूँ।
8. वाह! तुम किस **वेबसाइट** से सीख रहे हो?
9. मैं एक **एप्लिकेशन** के जरिए सीख रहा हूँ, जो मेरे **स्मार्टफोन** पर है।

✤ In Hindi, the participle mode combines the action of a verb with the quality of an adjective to describe doing something, like "पढ़ते हुए" (while reading) in the context of arts.

1. **pāṭha** ke lie tum kaun sī **kitāba** paṛh rahe ho?
2. maiṁ eka **upanyāsa** paṛh rahā hūm̐, yaha **kālpanika** hai.
3. kyā tumheṁ **kavitā** paṛhanā pasam̐da hai?
4. hām̐, mujhe **kavitāem̐** aura **gair-kālpanika** sāhitya donoṁ pasam̐da haiṁ.
5. tum **citrakalā** yā **phoṭogrāphī** meṁ bhī ruci rakhte ho?
6. mujhe **citra** banānā aura **gānā** bahuta pasam̐da hai.
7. maiṁ bhī, maiṁ inṭaraneta para **onlāina citrakalā** sīkh rahā hūm̐.
8. vāha! tum kisa **vebasāiṭa** se sīkh rahe ho?
9. maiṁ eka **eplikeśana** ke jarie sīkh rahā hūm̐, jo mere **smārṭaphōna** para hai.

1. **Text** Which **book** are you reading for the lesson?
2. I am reading a **novel**, it is **fictional**.
3. Do you like reading **poetry**?
4. Yes, I like both **poems** and **non-fiction** literature.
5. Are you also interested in **painting** or **photography**?
6. I really enjoy **drawing** and **singing**.
7. Me too, I am learning **online painting** on the internet.
8. Wow! Which **website** are you learning from?
9. I am learning through an **application** on my **smartphone**.

✤ The National Museum in New Delhi houses the only painting of the Mughal Emperor Akbar holding the Quran.

दिन 69: यात्रा और स्थान II

1. **हवाई अड्डा** पर जाने के लिए **टैक्सी** कहाँ मिलेगी?
2. **रेलवे स्टेशन** के पास ही मिल जाएगी।
3. मुझे **होटल** में जाना है या **युवा आवास** में?
4. **होटल** अच्छा रहेगा।
5. **सराय** में रुकना कैसा रहेगा?
6. वह भी ठीक है, पर **होटल** ज्यादा सुविधाजनक है।
7. मेरा **सामान** बहुत है, **बैकपैक** और **सूटकेस** दोनों।
8. कोई बात नहीं, **टैक्सी** में जगह होगी।
9. **दूतावास** जाने के लिए कितने **नोट** लगेंगे?
10. शायद कुछ **सिक्के** और **नोट**। **एटीएम** से निकाल लेना।

✤ In Hindi, to express an action as ongoing or habitual during travel or at a place, add "-ing" to the verb in English, but in Hindi, use the suffix "-ते हुए" for masculine subjects and "-ती हुई" for feminine subjects.

1. **havā'ī aḍḍā** par jāne ke lie **ṭaiksi** kahām̐ milegī?
2. **relve stēśan** ke pās hī mil jā'egī.
3. mujhe **hoṭal** meṃ jānā hai yā **yuvā āvās** meṃ?
4. **hoṭal** acchā rahegā.
5. **sarāy** meṃ ruknā kaisā rahegā?
6. vah bhī ṭhīk hai, par **hoṭal** jyādā suvidhājanak hai.
7. merā **sāmān** bahut hai, **baikpaik** aur **sūṭkēs** donoṃ.
8. koī bāt nahīṃ, **ṭaiksi** meṃ jagah hogī.
9. **dūtāvās** jāne ke lie kitne **noṭ** lagenge?
10. śāyad kuch **sikkē** aur **noṭ**. **ēṭīēm** se nikāl lenā.

DAY 69: TRAVEL AND PLACES II

1. Where can I find a **taxi** to go to the **airport**?
2. You'll find one near the **railway station**.
3. Should I go to a **hotel** or a **youth hostel**?
4. A **hotel** would be better.
5. How about staying at an **inn**?
6. That's fine too, but a **hotel** is more convenient.
7. I have a lot of **luggage**, both a **backpack** and a **suitcase**.
8. No problem, there will be space in the **taxi**.
9. How many **bills** will I need to go to the **embassy**?
10. Maybe a few **coins** and **bills**. Just withdraw from an **ATM**.

✤ In Varanasi, it's believed that a single dip in the Ganges can wash away a lifetime of sins.

दिन 70: संख्याएँ 11-20

1. क्या आपको पता है होटल से रेलवे स्टेशन कितनी दूर है?
2. हां, लगभग **चौदह** किलोमीटर है।
3. टैक्सी से कितना समय लगेगा?
4. अगर ट्रैफिक कम है तो **बीस** मिनट लगेंगे।
5. मौसम का पूर्वानुमान कैसा है?
6. आज थोड़ा नम है, लेकिन गरज और बिजली की संभावना नहीं है।
7. अच्छा, मैं एक टैक्सी बुक करता हूँ। क्या होटल में इंटरनेट है?
8. हां, वेबसाइट पर एप्लिकेशन के जरिए ऑनलाइन बुक कर सकते हैं।
9. शुक्रिया, मैं अपने स्मार्टफोन से बुक करता हूँ।

✤ In Hindi, when counting from 11 to 20, the numbers behave like adjectives and must agree in gender with the nouns they describe.

1. kyā āpko patā hai hoṭal se relve stēśan kitanī dūr hai?
2. hām̐, lagbhag **caudah** kilomīṭar hai.
3. ṭaikśī se kitanā samay lagegā?
4. agar ṭræphik kam hai to **bīs** minaṭ lagem̐ge.
5. mausam kā pūrvānumān kaisā hai?
6. āj thoṛā nam hai, lekin garaj aur bijalī kī sambhāvanā nahīṃ hai.
7. acchā, mā͡ī ek ṭaikśī buk karatā hūm̐. kyā hoṭal meṃ inṭarneṭ hai?
8. hām̐, vebasāiṭ par æplikeśan ke jariye onlāin buk kar sakte haim̐.
9. śukriyā, mā͡ī apane smārṭaphon se buk karatā hūm̐.

1. Do you know how far the railway station is from the hotel?
2. Yes, it's about **fourteen** kilometers.
3. How long will it take by taxi?
4. If the traffic is light, it will take **twenty** minutes.
5. What's the weather forecast like?
6. Today is a bit humid, but there's no chance of thunder and lightning.
7. Okay, I'll book a taxi. Is there internet in the hotel?
8. Yes, you can book online through the application on the website.
9. Thank you, I'll book it from my smartphone.

✤ In traditional Indian art, the number 108 is considered sacred and often depicted, symbolizing the universe's completeness.

CHALLENGE NO. 7

ENGAGE IN A 15-MINUTE CONVERSATION IN HINDI ON EVERYDAY TOPICS.

"सीखने में धैर्य रखें, सफलता आपके कदम चूमेगी।"

"Be patient in learning, success will kiss your feet."

दिन 71: 21 से 30 तक की संख्याएँ

1. आज कितनी तारीख है? **इक्कीस** मार्च है।
2. तुमने कितनी किताबें पढ़ीं? मैंने **बाईस** किताबें पढ़ीं।
3. तुम्हारी पसंदीदा किताब कौन सी है? मेरी पसंदीदा किताब **एक उपन्यास** है।
4. कल रात को क्या हुआ था? कल रात **आंधी** आई थी।
5. तुमने खाने में क्या बनाया? मैंने **पास्ता** बनाया था।
6. तुमने उसमें क्या डाला? मैंने **मक्खन** और **काली मिर्च** डाली।

✤ In Hindi, when using numbers from 21 to 30 in sentences, the noun following the number changes to its oblique form due to the grammatical notion of diathesis.

1. āja kitanī tārīkha hai? **ikkīsa** mārca hai.
2. tumne kitanī kitābeṁ paṛhīṁ? mainne **bāīsa** kitābeṁ paṛhīṁ.
3. tumhārī pasandīdā kitāba kaun sī hai? merī pasandīdā kitāba **eka upanyāsa** hai.
4. kala rāta ko kyā huā thā? kala rāta **āndhī** ā'ī thī.
5. tumne khāne meṁ kyā banāyā? mainne **pāstā** banāyā thā.
6. tumne usmeṁ kyā ḍālā? mainne **makhaṇa** aura **kālī mirca** ḍālī.

1. What's the date today? **The twenty-first** of March.
2. How many books have you read? I have read **twenty-two** books.
3. What's your favorite book? My favorite book is **a novel**.
4. What happened last night? There was **a storm** last night.
5. What did you make for dinner? I made **pasta**.
6. What did you add to it? I added **butter** and **black pepper**.

✤ In ancient India, mathematicians like Aryabhata used poetry and verse to teach complex mathematical concepts, blending art with science.

1. **पंचांग** देखकर आज का **टाइमटेबल** बताओ।
2. आज **शुक्रवार** है, **त्योहार** का दिन।
3. हां, **परंपरा** के अनुसार **संग्रहालय** जाएंगे।
4. **संस्कृति** और **इतिहास** सीखने को मिलेगा।
5. **आदिवासी** कला भी देखेंगे।
6. **पर्यटक** के लिए बहुत **आरामदायक** होगा।
7. होटल से **रेलवे स्टेशन** कैसे जाएं?
8. **टैक्सी** से जाना सबसे अच्छा है।
9. ठीक है, चलो तैयार होते हैं।

✣ Valency in Hindi grammar refers to the number of arguments a verb can have, such as one for intransitive verbs and two or more for transitive verbs.

1. **pañcāṅga** dekhakar āja kā **ṭaimaṭebala** batao.
2. āja **śukravāra** hai, **tyohāra** kā dina.
3. hāṃ, **paramparā** ke anusāra **saṅgrahālaya** jāeṅge.
4. **saṃskṛti** aura **itihāsa** sīkhane ko milegā.
5. **ādivāsī** kalā bhī dekheṅge.
6. **paryaṭaka** ke liye bahuta **ārāmadāyaka** hogā.
7. hoṭala se **relave seṭhana** kaise jāeṅ?
8. **ṭaiksi** se jānā sabase acchā hai.
9. ṭhīka hai, calo taiyāra hote haiṃ.

1. Check the **almanac** and tell me today's **timetable**.
2. Today is **Friday**, a day of **festivals**.
3. Yes, according to **tradition**, we will go to the **museum**.
4. We will learn about **culture** and **history**.
5. We will also see **tribal** art.
6. It will be very **comfortable** for **tourists**.
7. How do we get to the **railway station** from the hotel?
8. Taking a **taxi** is the best way.
9. Alright, let's get ready.

✣ In India, there's a festival where people throw tomatoes at each other for fun, known as the "Tomatina" inspired event.

दिन 73: रसोई और खाना पकाने II

1. आज तुमने क्या बनाया?
2. मैंने **ओवन** में केक बनाया।
3. **फ्रिज** में सब्जियां हैं?
4. हां, और **फ्रीजर** में आइसक्रीम भी है।
5. तुम **थाली** में क्या खा रहे हो?
6. मैं **तवा** पर रोटी बना रहा हूँ।
7. **चम्मच** कहाँ है?
8. वह **कांटे** और **चाकू** के पास है।
9. **टोस्टर** से ब्रेड निकालो।
10. ठीक है, मैं अभी निकालता हूँ।

✣ In Hindi, verbs change form based on whether the action directly affects an object (transitive) or not (intransitive), so for cooking actions, remember to use the correct verb form depending on if you're specifying what is being cooked (transitive) or simply stating the act of cooking (intransitive).

1. āja tumane kyā banāyā?
2. mainne **ovan** men keka banāyā.
3. **phrija** men sabjiyā̃ haiṁ?
4. hā̃, aura **phrījara** men ā'iskrīma bhī hai.
5. tum **thālī** men kyā khā rahe ho?
6. main **tavā** para rōṭī banā rahā hū̃.
7. **cammaca** kahā̃ hai?
8. vaha **kāṇṭe** aura **cākū** ke pāsa hai.
9. **ṭosṭara** se breḍa nikālo.
10. ṭhīka hai, main abhī nikālatā hū̃.

DAY 73: COOKING AND KITCHEN II

1. What did you make today?
2. I made a cake in the **oven**.
3. Are there vegetables in the **fridge**?
4. Yes, and there's also ice cream in the **freezer**.
5. What are you eating on your **plate**?
6. I'm making roti on the **griddle**.
7. Where is the **spoon**?
8. It's near the **fork** and **knife**.
9. Take the bread out of the **toaster**.
10. Okay, I'll take it out now.

✣ MasterChef India not only showcases the diversity of Indian cuisine but also often leads to a revival of forgotten regional dishes.

दिन 74: चिकित्सा और स्वास्थ्य II

1. **बुखार** है, **खांसी** भी है।
2. **सिरदर्द** से राहत नहीं मिल रही।
3. **एलर्जी** की **गोली** ली?
4. हां, पर **तरल** दवा बेहतर होती है।
5. **पर्चा** दिखाओ, **फार्मेसी** जाना होगा।
6. **क्लिनिक** जाने का समय है।
7. **दांत दर्द** के लिए डॉक्टर को दिखाना पड़ेगा।
8. हां, चलो जल्दी करते हैं।
9. ठीक है, चलते हैं।

✤ In Hindi, verbs related to feeling sick, like "बीमार पड़ना" (to fall ill), don't need a direct object to make sense, showing intransitivity.

1. **bukhāra** hai, **khāṃsī** bhī hai.
2. **sirdard** se rāhat nahīṃ mil rahī.
3. **elarjī** kī **golī** lī?
4. hāṃ, par **taral** davā behtar hotī hai.
5. **parcā** dikhāo, **phārmesī** jānā hogā.
6. **klinik** jāne kā samaya hai.
7. **dāṃt dard** ke lie ḍākṭar ko dikhānā paṛegā.
8. hāṃ, calo jaldī karate haiṃ.
9. ṭhīk hai, calate haiṃ.

DAY 74: MEDICAL AND HEALTH II

1. **Fever** is there, **cough** as well.
2. **Headache** relief is not coming.
3. Took the **allergy pill**?
4. Yes, but **liquid** medicine is better.
5. Show the **prescription**, need to go to the **pharmacy**.
6. It's time to go to the **clinic**.
7. For **toothache**, need to see a doctor.
8. Yes, let's hurry up.
9. Alright, let's go.

✤ In India, Kalyan Banerjee co-founded the Rotary Club of Vapi, which played a pivotal role in India's fight against polio, leading to the country being declared polio-free in 2014.

दिन 75: शिक्षा और सीखना

1. आज **स्कूल** में क्या **पाठ** पढ़ाएंगे?
2. क्या हम **विषय** 'इतिहास' पर चर्चा कर सकते हैं?
3. बिल्कुल, इतिहास में **परंपराओं** और **त्योहारों** के बारे में पढ़ेंगे।
4. **होमवर्क** के लिए क्या करना होगा?
5. **किताब** से तीन अध्याय पढ़ो और सारांश लिखो।
6. **परीक्षा** कब होगी?
7. **परीक्षा** का **टाइमटेबल** अगले सप्ताह बताऊंगा।
8. ठीक है, मैं **कलम** और **किताब** लेकर तैयार रहूंगा।
9. शाबाश! अच्छी तैयारी करना।

✤ In Hindi, to express reflexivity, we add "-आप" to the verb, indicating the action is done by the subject to themselves, as in "वह खुद को पढ़ाता है" (He teaches himself).

1. Aaj school mein kya paath padhaayenge?
2. Kya hum vishay 'Itihaas' par charcha kar sakte hain?
3. Bilkul, itihaas mein paramparao aur tyoharon ke baare mein padhenge.
4. Homework ke liye kya karna hoga?
5. Kitab se teen adhyaay padho aur saaransh likho.
6. Pariksha kab hogi?
7. Pariksha ka timetable agle saptaah bataaunga.
8. Theek hai, main kalam aur kitab lekar taiyaar rahunga.
9. Shaabash! Acchi taiyari karna.

1. What **lesson** will be taught in **school** today?
2. Can we discuss the **subject** 'History'?
3. Absolutely, we will learn about **traditions** and **festivals** in history.
4. What will we have to do for **homework**?
5. Read three chapters from the **book** and write a summary.
6. When will the **exam** be?
7. I will tell you the **exam timetable** next week.
8. Okay, I will be ready with my **pen** and **book**.
9. Well done! Prepare well.

✤ India's ancient Nalanda University, established in the 5th century, was one of the world's first residential universities, attracting students from across the globe.

दिन 76: पैसा और शॉपिंग II

1. **एटीएम** से पैसे निकालना है?
2. हां, मुझे **नकद** चाहिए। **क्रेडिट कार्ड** से नहीं चलेगा।
3. **कीमत** ज्यादा है या **सस्ती**?
4. थोड़ा **महंगा** है, पर **मुद्रा** की **विनिमय दर** अच्छी है।
5. **रसीद** मिलेगी?
6. हां, और अगर सामान पसंद नहीं आया तो **वापसी** भी।
7. अच्छा है। चलो फिर **शॉपिंग** करते हैं।

✣ In Hindi, to express reciprocity during shopping, we often use the verb "देना" (to give) and "लेना" (to take), as in "मैंने दुकानदार को पैसे दिए और उसने मुझे सामान दिया" (I gave money to the shopkeeper and he gave me the goods).

1. **ēṭīēma** se paise nikālanā hai?
2. hāṁ, mujhe **nakada** cāhie. **kreḍiṭa kārḍa** se nahīṁ calegā.
3. **kīmata** jyādā hai yā **sastī**?
4. ṭhoḍā **mahangā** hai, par **mudrā** kī **vinimaya dara** acchī hai.
5. **rasīda** milegī?
6. hāṁ, aura agar sāmāna pasanda nahīṁ āyā to **vāpasī** bhī.
7. acchā hai. calo phira **śŏpiṅga** karte haiṁ.

DAY 76: MONEY AND SHOPPING II

1. Need to withdraw money from the **ATM**?
2. Yes, I need **cash**. **Credit card** won't do.
3. Is the **price** high or **cheap**?
4. It's a bit **expensive**, but the **exchange rate** for the **currency** is good.
5. Will I get a **receipt**?
6. Yes, and if you don't like the item, there's also a **return** option.
7. That's good. Let's go **shopping** then.

✤ Bollywood movies often depict lavish weddings that significantly boost local economies by inspiring similar real-life celebrations.

दिन 77: बाहर खाना II

1. आज **रेस्टोरेंट** में क्या खाएंगे?
2. **मेन्यू** में **स्टार्टर** के लिए कुछ देखते हैं।
3. **सलाद** और **सैंडविच** कैसा रहेगा?
4. अच्छा है। और **मुख्य व्यंजन** में?
5. **टोस्ट** और **जैम** लेंगे।
6. ठीक है, और **मिठाई** में **चॉकलेट** हो जाए?
7. हां, बिलकुल। चलो ऑर्डर करते हैं।
8. भुगतान कैसे करेंगे? **क्रेडिट कार्ड** या **नकद**?
9. **क्रेडिट कार्ड** से, और **रसीद** भी लेनी है।

✤ In Hindi, the agent (the doer of an action) in sentences with passive voice is marked by the postposition 'द्वारा' (dwara).

1. āja **resṭōrēṁṭa** mẽ kyā khāẽge?
2. **menyū** mẽ **sṭārṭara** ke lie kucha dekhte haiṁ.
3. **salāda** aura **saiṁḍavica** kaisā rahegā?
4. acchā hai. aura **mukhya vyañjana** mẽ?
5. **ṭōsṭa** aura **jāma** leṁge.
6. ṭhīka hai, aura **miṭhāī** mẽ **cŏkalaṭa** hō jāe?
7. hāṁ, bilakula. calō ŏrḍara karate haiṁ.
8. bhugatāna kaise kareṁge? **kreḍiṭa kārḍa** yā **nakaḍa**?
9. **kreḍiṭa kārḍa** se, aura **rasīḍa** bhī lenī hai.

DAY 77: EATING OUT II

1. What shall we eat at the **restaurant** today?
2. Let's look at the **menu** for some **starters**.
3. How about **salad** and **sandwiches**?
4. Sounds good. And for the **main course**?
5. We'll have **toast** and **jam**.
6. Okay, and for **dessert**, shall we go for **chocolate**?
7. Yes, absolutely. Let's place the order.
8. How will we pay? **Credit card** or **cash**?
9. With a **credit card**, and we need to get the **receipt** as well.

✤ In India, the ancient art of palm leaf manuscript restoration is a revered tradition, keeping centuries-old texts alive for future generations.

दिन 78: घर और फर्नीचर II

1. यह सोफा कितने का है?
2. वह मेज और कुर्सियां देखो, बहुत सुंदर हैं।
3. मेरे बिस्तर के पास एक खिड़की है।
4. क्या तुम दरवाजा बंद कर सकते हो?
5. मेरे घर में नया ओवन है।
6. फ्रिज खाली है, खाना खत्म हो गया।
7. रात में लैंप जलाओ।
8. टेलीविजन पर क्या आ रहा है?

✤ In Hindi, to say you are doing something with an object, like sitting on a chair, add 'से' (se) after the noun, as in 'कुर्सी से' (kursi se - with a chair).

1. yah sopha kitane kā hai?
2. vah mez aur kursiyā̃ dekho, bahut sundar hain.
3. mere bistar ke pās ek khiṛakī hai.
4. kyā tum daravāzā band kar sakte ho?
5. mere ghar meṃ nayā ovan hai.
6. frij khālī hai, khānā khatm ho gayā.
7. rāt meṃ laimp jalāo.
8. ṭelīvijan par kyā ā rahā hai?

1. How much is this sofa?
2. Look at that table and chairs, they are very beautiful.
3. There is a window next to my bed.
4. Can you close the door?
5. There is a new oven in my house.
6. The fridge is empty, the food is all gone.
7. Turn on the lamp at night.
8. What's on television?

✤ In ancient India, Vastu Shastra, an architectural science, guided the design of buildings to harmonize with nature's energy.

दिन 79: मौसम II

1. **जलवायु** पूर्वानुमान क्या है?
2. आज **नम** मौसम है, **गरज** के साथ **बिजली** भी है।
3. क्या **तूफान** आने वाला है?
4. हां, **चक्रवात** की संभावना है।
5. **बवंडर** तो नहीं आएगा?
6. नहीं, पर **भूकंप** का कोई खतरा नहीं है।
7. और **ज्वालामुखी**?
8. ज्वालामुखी सक्रिय नहीं है, चिंता न करें।
9. ठीक है, मैं खिड़की बंद कर देता हूं।

✤ In Hindi, to describe the weather, you often use an adverbial phrase after the verb, like "बारिश तेज़ी से हो रही है" (The rain is falling heavily), where "तेज़ी से" (heavily) is the adverbial phrase describing how the rain is falling.

1. **jalavāyu** pūrvānumān kyā hai?
2. āj **nam** mausam hai, **garaj** ke sāth **bijlī** bhī hai.
3. kyā **tūfān** āne vālā hai?
4. hāṁ, **cakravāt** kī sambhāvanā hai.
5. **bavaṇḍar** to nahīṁ āegā?
6. nahīṁ, par **bhūkamp** kā koī khatrā nahīṁ hai.
7. aur **jvālāmukhī**?
8. jvālāmukhī sakriy nahīṁ hai, cintā na karen.
9. ṭhīk hai, maiṁ khiḍkī band kar detā hūṁ.

DAY 79: WEATHER II

1. What is the **climate** forecast?
2. Today is **humid** weather, with **thunder** and **lightning** as well.
3. Is a **storm** coming?
4. Yes, there is a possibility of a **cyclone**.
5. No **tornado**, right?
6. No, but there is no risk of an **earthquake**.
7. And **volcanoes**?
8. The volcano is not active, do not worry.
9. Alright, I'll close the window.

✤ In India, it's believed that if a lizard makes a noise during a rainstorm, it's a sign of good luck and prosperity.

दिन ८०: शौक और हॉबीज II

1. क्या तुम्हें **सिनेमा** देखना पसंद है?
2. हां, मुझे **नाटक** और **संगीत** वाली फिल्में अच्छी लगती हैं।
3. मुझे **ट्रेकिंग** और **स्कीइंग** का शौक है।
4. वाह! मैं **तैराकी** और **स्नोबोर्डिंग** करना चाहता हूँ।
5. **नृत्य** और **खेलना** भी मजेदार होते हैं।
6. हां, और **गीत** गाना भी।
7. तुमने **मॉल** में नया **जैकेट** खरीदा?
8. नहीं, मैंने **किराने की दुकान** से सामान लिया।
9. अच्छा, चलो कभी **रेस्टोरेंट** में **मुख्य व्यंजन** खाने चलें।

✣ In Hindi, to express an action that took place at a specific time, add the time complement after the verb, for example, "मैंने सुबह तैराकी की।" (I swam in the morning.)

1. kyā tumhẽ **sinemā** dekhnā pasaṅd hai?
2. hā̃ṁ, mujhe **nāṭak** aur **saṅgīt** vālī philmeṃ acchī lagtī haṃ.
3. mujhe **ṭrekig** aur **skīig** kā śauk hai.
4. vāh! maiṃ **tairākī** aur **snoborḍig** karnā cāhtā hū̃ṁ.
5. **nṛtya** aur **khelnā** bhī majedār hote haṃ.
6. hā̃ṁ, aur **gīt** gānā bhī.
7. tumne **māl** meṃ nayā **jækeṭ** kharīdā?
8. nahī̃ṁ, maine **kirāne kī dukān** se sāmān liyā.
9. acchā, calo kabhī **resṭorẽṭ** meṃ **mukhya vyañjan** khāne caleṃ.

DAY 80: LEISURE AND HOBBIES II

1. Do you like watching **movies**?
2. Yes, I like films with **drama** and **music**.
3. I enjoy **trekking** and **skiing**.
4. Wow! I want to do **swimming** and **snowboarding**.
5. **Dancing and playing** are also fun.
6. Yes, and singing **songs** too.
7. Did you buy a new **jacket** at the **mall**?
8. No, I got some stuff from the **grocery store**.
9. Alright, let's go have **main dishes** at a **restaurant** sometime.

✤ In India, kite flying transcends a mere hobby, uniting millions during festivals like Makar Sankranti, where the sky becomes a canvas of vibrant colors.

CHALLENGE NO. 8

SPEAK ONLY IN HINDI FOR AN HOUR.

"भाषाओं की विविधता, संस्कृति की समृद्धि।"

"The diversity of languages is the richness of culture."

दिन 81: परिवहन II

1. **रेलगाड़ी** से जाना है?
2. नहीं, **बस** से जाएंगे।
3. **कार** में जगह है?
4. हाँ, पर **हवाई जहाज** तेज़ है।
5. **साइकिल** से जा सकते हैं?
6. नहीं, **ट्रक** से बेहतर है।
7. **जहाज** पर चलें?
8. **नाव** से मज़ा आएगा।
9. **मेट्रो** या **ट्राम**?
10. **मेट्रो** जल्दी है।

✤ In Hindi, to indicate where an action is happening, we often place the adverb of place after the verb, for example, "वह स्कूल जाता है" (He goes to school), where "स्कूल" is the adverbial of place indicating where the action of going is directed.

1. **relagāṛī** se jānā hai?
2. nahīṁ, **bas** se jā.eṅge.
3. **kār** meṁ jagah hai?
4. hām̐, par **havāī jahāj** tez hai.
5. **saikil** se jā sakte haiṁ?
6. nahīṁ, **ṭrak** se behatar hai.
7. **jahāj** par caleṁ?
8. **nāv** se mazā āegā.
9. **meṭro** yā **ṭrām**?
10. **meṭro** jaldī hai.

DAY 81: TRANSPORT II

1. Going by **train**?
2. No, we'll go by **bus**.
3. Is there room in the **car**?
4. Yes, but the **airplane** is faster.
5. Can we go by **bicycle**?
6. No, **truck** is better.
7. Shall we go on a **ship**?
8. **Boat** will be more fun.
9. **Metro** or **tram**?
10. **Metro** is faster.

✣ India's first train ran between Mumbai and Thane in 1853, marking a revolutionary shift in transportation.

दिन 82: प्रकृति और भूगोल II

1. **पहाड़** पर चढ़ना है?
2. हां, और **नदी** के पास **झील** भी देखनी है।
3. **महासागर** किनारे **समुद्र तट** पर जाएंगे?
4. जी, फिर **रेगिस्तान** में सफारी करेंगे।
5. **जंगल** में जानवर देखने का मन है?
6. हां, और **वन** में पक्षी भी।
7. **घाटी** में पिकनिक कैसा रहेगा?
8. अच्छा विचार है। **द्वीप** पर भी जाना है।
9. चलो, यात्रा का **टाइमटेबल** बनाते हैं।

✤ In Hindi, to express the cause or reason for an action, we use the structure "के कारण" or "से" after the noun or pronoun indicating the cause.

1. **pahāṛ** par caṛhnā hai?
2. hāṃ, aura **nadī** ke pās **jhīl** bhī dekhnī hai.
3. **mahāsāgar** kināre **samudra taṭ** par jāeṅge?
4. jī, phira **registān** meṃ saphārī kareṅge.
5. **jaṅgal** meṃ jānavar dekhne kā mana hai?
6. hāṃ, aura **van** meṃ pakṣī bhī.
7. **ghāṭī** meṃ piknik kaisā rahegā?
8. acchā vicāra hai. **dvīp** par bhī jānā hai.
9. calo, yātrā kā **ṭaimṭebal** banāte haiṃ.

1. Want to climb the **mountain**?
2. Yes, and also want to see the **lake** near the **river**.
3. Shall we go to the **beach** by the **ocean**?
4. Yes, then we'll do a safari in the **desert**.
5. Feel like seeing animals in the **jungle**?
6. Yes, and birds in the **forest** too.
7. How about a picnic in the **valley**?
8. Good idea. Want to go to the **island** as well.
9. Let's make a **timetable** for the trip.

✤ India's first national park was established in 1936 as Hailey National Park, now known as Jim Corbett National Park, to protect the endangered Bengal tiger.

1. **कल** सुबह मैंने तैराकी की थी।
2. **आज** दोपहर को मैं पहाड़ पर ट्रेकिंग करूंगा।
3. **कल** शाम को तुम नदी के पास गए थे ना?
4. हां, **अभी** मैं सोफे पर बैठकर उसकी तस्वीरें देख रहा हूं।
5. **सुबह** मैंने फ्रिज से ठंडा पानी निकाला था।
6. **दोपहर** को मैं थाली में खाना खाऊंगा।
7. **शाम** को हम सिनेमा जाएंगे।
8. **रात** को क्या खाना बनाओगे?
9. **आधी रात** को मैं सो जाऊंगा।

✤ In Hindi, to express purpose, we often use "के लिए" after the noun or pronoun, as in "मैं बाजार खाना खरीदने के लिए जा रहा हूँ" (I am going to the market to buy food).

1. **kala** subaha mainne tairākī kī thī.
2. **āja** dopahara ko main pahāṛa para ṭrekiṁ̐ga karūṁ̐gā.
3. **kala** śāma ko tuma nadī ke pāsa ga'e the nā?
4. hāṁ̐, **abhī** main sofe para baiṭhakara usakī tasvīreṁ̐ dekha rahā hūṁ̐.
5. **subaha** mainne frija se ṭhaṇḍā pānī nikālā thā.
6. **dopahara** ko main thālī meṁ̐ khānā khā'ūṁ̐gā.
7. **śāma** ko hama sinemā jā'eṁ̐ge.
8. **rāta** ko kyā khānā banā'oge?
9. **ādhī rāta** ko main so jā'ūṁ̐gā.

1. **Yesterday** morning I went swimming.
2. **Today** afternoon I will go trekking on the mountain.
3. **Yesterday** evening you went near the river, right?
4. Yes, **now** I am sitting on the sofa looking at its pictures.
5. **In the morning** I took out cold water from the fridge.
6. **In the afternoon** I will eat food on a plate.
7. **In the evening** we will go to the cinema.
8. **At night** what will you cook?
9. **At midnight** I will go to sleep.

✣ In many Indian households, the day begins with the ritual of drawing Rangoli, a colorful pattern made on the floor, to welcome good luck and positivity.

दिन 84: भावनाएँ III

1. आज सुबह मैं **अकेला** था, पर **संतुष्ट** था।
2. दोपहर में मुझे बुखार आया, मैं **परेशान** हो गया।
3. **डरा हुआ** नहीं, मैंने गोली ली और **आराम** महसूस किया।
4. कल मैं **प्रसन्न** था, क्योंकि मैंने साइकिल चलाई।
5. मेरी साइकिल की **लंबाई** और **ऊंचाई** सही है।
6. अभी मैं **गर्वित** हूँ, क्योंकि मैंने खुद साइकिल ठीक की।
7. लेकिन मैं **क्रोधित** हूँ, क्योंकि देर हो गई।
8. मैं **चिंतित** और **घबराया हुआ** हूँ, कहीं फिर बुखार न आ जाए।

✤ In Hindi, a relative clause, which provides additional information about a noun, is introduced by relative pronouns like "jo" (जो) for "who" or "which."

1. Āja subaha maiṁ **akelā** thā, para **santuṣṭa** thā.
2. Dopahara meṁ mujhe bukhāra āyā, maiṁ **pareśāna** ho gayā.
3. **Ḍarā huā** nahīṁ, maiṁne golī lī aura **ārāma** mahasūsa kiyā.
4. Kala maiṁ **prasanna** thā, kyoṅki maiṁne saikila calā'ī.
5. Merī saikila kī **laṁbā'ī** aura **ūṁcā'ī** sahī hai.
6. Abhī maiṁ **garvita** hūm̐, kyoṅki maiṁne khuda saikila ṭhīka kī.
7. Lekina maiṁ **krodhita** hūm̐, kyoṅki dera ho ga'ī.
8. Maiṁ **cintita** aura **ghabarāyā huā** hūm̐, kahīm̐ phira bukhāra na ā jā'e.

DAY 84: EMOTIONS III

1. This morning I was **alone**, but **content**.
2. In the afternoon, I got a fever, I became **worried**.
3. Not **scared**, I took a pill and felt **relaxed**.
4. Yesterday, I was **happy** because I rode my bicycle.
5. The **length** and **height** of my bicycle are just right.
6. Now, I am **proud** because I fixed the bicycle myself.
7. But I am **angry** because it's late.
8. I am **anxious** and **nervous**, fearing the fever might return.

✤ During the festival of Raksha Bandhan, sisters tie a rakhi (sacred thread) on their brothers' wrists, symbolizing a promise of protection and the deep emotional bond between them.

दिन 85: रंग और आकार

1. किताब का रंग लाल और नीला है।
2. पेन हरा है।
3. मेरा बैग काला और सफेद है।
4. टेबल गोल है और घड़ी वर्गाकार है।
5. मुझे गणित पसंद है, पर होमवर्क परेशानी करता है।
6. 'और' का उपयोग रंग और आकार जोड़ने के लिए किया जाता है।

✤ In Hindi, when describing colors and shapes together, use the conjunction "और" (aur) to connect them, like "लाल और गोल" (red and round).

1. Kitab ka rang lal aur neela hai.
2. Pen hara hai.
3. Mera bag kala aur safed hai.
4. Table gol aur ghadi vargakar hai.
5. Mujhe ganit pasand hai, par homework pareshan karta hai.
6. 'Aur' kā upayog rang aur ākār joḍne ke liye kiyā jātā hai.

DAY 85: COLORS AND SHAPES

1. The color of the book is red and blue.
2. The pen is green.
3. My bag is black and white.
4. The table is round, and the clock is square.
5. I like math, but homework is troublesome.
6. 'And' is used to join colors and shapes.

✣ In traditional Indian art, the lotus shape symbolizes purity and divine beauty.

दिन 86: संबंध

1. आज सोमवार है, तुम्हारा **परिवार** कैसा है?
2. अच्छा है, और तुम्हारे **दोस्त** और **सहकर्मी**?
3. सब ठीक हैं। कल मेरे **पड़ोसी** ने मुझे नीला फूल दिया।
4. वाह! मेरी **पत्नी** ने भी मुझे पीला गुलाब दिया।
5. तुम्हारे **चचेरे भाई** का क्या हाल है?
6. वह ठीक है, उसने अभी नया काला कोट खरीदा।
7. अच्छा, मेरे **पति** ने भी नया क्रेडिट कार्ड लिया।
8. मेरी **मंगेतर** ने एटीएम से नकद निकाला।
9. उम्मीद है उसने रसीद ली होगी।

✤ In Hindi, an adverbial clause often starts with conjunctions like "जब" (when), "क्योंकि" (because), or "अगर" (if) to show the relationship of time, reason, or condition between actions.

1. āja somavāra hai, tumhārā **parivāra** kaisā hai?
2. acchā hai, aura tumhāre **dosta** aura **sahakarmī**?
3. saba ṭhīka haiṃ. kala mere **paḍosī** ne mujhe nīlā phūla diyā.
4. vāha! merī **patnī** ne bhī mujhe pīlā gulāba diyā.
5. tumhāre **cacere bhāī** kā kyā hāla hai?
6. vaha ṭhīka hai, usane abhī nayā kālā koṭa kharīdā.
7. acchā, mere **pati** ne bhī nayā kreḍiṭa kārḍa liyā.
8. merī **maṅgetara** ne eṭīema se nakada nikālā.
9. um'mīda hai usane rasīda lī hogī.

1. Today is Monday, how is your **family**?
2. Good, and how about your **friends** and **colleagues**?
3. All is well. Yesterday, my **neighbor** gave me a blue flower.
4. Wow! My **wife** also gave me a yellow rose.
5. How is your **cousin** doing?
6. He's fine, he just bought a new black coat.
7. Oh, my **husband** also got a new credit card.
8. My **fiancé** withdrew cash from the ATM.
9. Hope they took the receipt.

✤ In ancient Indian literature, the epic Mahabharata portrays the deep bond of love and friendship between Lord Krishna and Arjuna, symbolizing divine support and human devotion.

दिन 87: कपड़े और सामान

1. **आज** सुबह तुमने क्या पहना है?
2. मैंने **जैकेट** और **जूते** पहने हैं।
3. और **टोपी** और **धूप का चश्मा**?
4. हाँ, वे भी पहने हैं। **शर्ट** और **पैंट** भी।
5. लड़कियां **स्कर्ट** और **हार** पहनती हैं न?
6. हाँ, और **बालियाँ** भी।
7. तुम **प्रसन्न** लग रहे हो।
8. हाँ, मैं **संतुष्ट** हूँ।
9. अच्छा है। चलो **रेस्टोरेंट** में **मिठाई** खाते हैं।

✤ In Hindi, to compare two items of clothing or accessories, use "से" (se) after the adjective, like "यह शर्ट उस शर्ट से बड़ी है" (This shirt is bigger than that shirt).

1. **āja** subaha tumane kyā pahanā hai?
2. maine **jaikēṭa** aura **jūtē** pahanē haiṁ.
3. aura **ṭōpī** aura **dhūpa kā caśmā**?
4. hām̐, vē bhī pahanē haiṁ. **śarṭa** aura **paiṇṭa** bhī.
5. laṛakiyām̐ **skarṭa** aura **hāra** pahanatī haiṁ na?
6. hām̐, aura **bāliyām̐** bhī.
7. tum **prasanna** laga rahē hō.
8. hām̐, main **santuṣṭa** hūm̐.
9. acchā hai. calō **rēsṭōrēm̐ṭa** mēṁ **miṭhāī** khātē haiṁ.

1. **What** did you wear this morning?
2. I wore a **jacket** and **shoes**.
3. And a **hat** and **sunglasses**?
4. Yes, those too. A **shirt** and **pants** as well.
5. Girls wear **skirts** and **necklaces**, right?
6. Yes, and **earrings** too.
7. You look **happy**.
8. Yes, I am **satisfied**.
9. That's good. Let's go eat **dessert** at the **restaurant**.

✣ In ancient India, the art of dyeing clothes with indigo, a vibrant blue dye, was so advanced that it became a coveted export in Roman markets.

दिन 88: प्रौद्योगिकी और मीडिया II

1. **टेलीविज़न** पर क्या देख रहे हो?
2. **समाचार** चैनल है। **रिमोट कंट्रोल** दो, मुझे **कंप्यूटर** पर काम करना है।
3. **स्मार्टफोन** से **ईमेल** भेज दिया?
4. हां, और **सोशल मीडिया** पर भी अपडेट कर दिया।
5. **ऑनलाइन** खबरें तेज़ होती हैं।
6. सच है, लेकिन **रेडियो** की अपनी बात है।
7. तुम्हारा **स्मार्टफोन** कहाँ है?
8. सोफे के पास, **मेज़** पर।
9. अच्छा, मैं **कंप्यूटर** चालू करता हूँ।

✤ In Hindi, to express a cause or reason, we use "क्योंकि" (kyonki) at the beginning of a clause, similar to "because" in English.

1. **ṭēlīvijan** par kyā dēkh rahē hō?
2. **samācār** cainal hai. **rimōṭ kanṭrōl** dō, mujhē **kampyūṭar** par kām karanā hai.
3. **smārṭphōn** sē **īmēl** bhēj diyā?
4. hāṁ, aura **sōśal mīḍiyā** par bhī apaḍēṭ kar diyā.
5. **anlain** khabarēṁ tēz hōtī haiṁ̐.
6. sac hai, lēkin **rēḍiyō** kī apanī bāt hai.
7. tumhārā **smārṭphōn** kahāṁ̐ hai?
8. sōphē kē pās, **mēz** par.
9. acchā, maiṁ **kampyūṭar** cālū karatā hūṁ̐.

1. **What are you watching** on TV?
2. It's a **news** channel. Give me the **remote control**, I need to work on the **computer**.
3. Did you send the **email** from your **smartphone**?
4. Yes, and also updated on **social media**.
5. **Online** news is faster.
6. True, but there's something special about the **radio**.
7. Where is your **smartphone**?
8. Near the sofa, on the **table**.
9. Alright, I'll turn on the **computer**.

✣ Bollywood was so named because Bombay (now Mumbai) was the hub of Hindi cinema and it merged with Hollywood, showcasing the global influence of technology on film.

दिन 89: खाना और पेय II

1. आज खाने में क्या बनाएंगे?
2. **सब्जियां** और **फल** का सलाद कैसा रहेगा?
3. अच्छा विचार है। **मांस** नहीं खाएंगे?
4. नहीं, आज सिर्फ शाकाहारी खाना है।
5. पीने के लिए क्या लेंगे? **सोडा** या **जूस**?
6. **पानी** ही ठीक रहेगा।
7. ठीक है, और चाय-कॉफ़ी?
8. बाद में **चाय** पीएंगे। **कॉफ़ी** नहीं।
9. और **दूध**?
10. हाँ, रात को **दूध** पीएंगे।

✤ If you eat spicy food (अगर आप मसालेदार खाना खाते हैं), you will need water (तो आपको पानी की ज़रूरत पड़ेगी).

1. āja khāne mẽ kyā banāẽge?
2. **sabzīyā̃** aura **phala** kā salāda kaisā rahegā?
3. acchā vicāra hai. **mā̃sa** nahī̃ khāẽge?
4. nahī̃, āja sirpha śākāhārī khānā hai.
5. pīne ke lie kyā leṅge? **soḍā** yā **jūsa**?
6. **pānī** hī ṭhīka rahegā.
7. ṭhīka hai, aura cāya-kŏphī?
8. bāda meṃ **cāya** pīẽge. **kŏphī** nahī̃.
9. aura **dūdha**?
10. hā̃, rāta ko **dūdha** pīẽge.

1. What should we make for dinner today?
2. How about a **vegetable** and **fruit** salad?
3. That's a good idea. Won't we have **meat**?
4. No, today we'll only have vegetarian food.
5. What would you like to drink? **Soda** or **juice**?
6. **Water** will be fine.
7. Okay, and about tea or coffee?
8. We'll have **tea** later. Not **coffee**.
9. And **milk**?
10. Yes, we'll have **milk** at night.

✤ In India, the beloved street food "pani puri" has different names across regions, such as "golgappa" in North India and "phuchka" in West Bengal.

1. **घर** में कितने **कमरे** हैं?
2. चार **कमरे**, एक **बाथरूम**, और एक **रसोई**.
3. **लिविंग रूम** कैसा है?
4. बहुत बड़ा है और **बालकनी** भी है.
5. **बगीचा** और **आँगन** है?
6. हाँ, और एक छोटा **गैराज** भी.
7. अच्छा है! **अपार्टमेंट** में **बालकनी** से क्या दिखता है?
8. **बालकनी** से पार्क और शहर दिखते हैं.
9. वाह! मैं **उत्साहित** हूँ.

✤ In Hindi, to express an action that will happen before another, we use the temporal clause with "जब" (jab) for "when" followed by the future tense in the main clause.

1. **ghara** mẽ kitane **kamare** haĩ?
2. cāra **kamare**, eka **bāthrūma**, aura eka **rasoī**.
3. **liviṅga rūma** kaisā hai?
4. bahuta baṛā hai aura **bālakanī** bhī hai.
5. **bagīcā** aura **ā̃gana** hai?
6. hā̃, aura eka choṭā **gairāja** bhī.
7. acchā hai! **apārṭamẽṭa** mẽ **bālakanī** se kyā dikhata hai?
8. **bālakanī** se pārka aura śahara dikhate haĩ.
9. vāha! maiṃ **utsāhita** hū̃.

1. How many **rooms** are there in the **house**?
2. Four **rooms**, one **bathroom**, and one **kitchen**.
3. What's the **living room** like?
4. It's very big and has a **balcony** too.
5. Is there a **garden** and **courtyard**?
6. Yes, and a small **garage** as well.
7. Great! What can you see from the **balcony** of the **apartment**?
8. From the **balcony**, you can see the park and the city.
9. Wow! I'm **excited**.

✤ The Jaisalmer Havelis in India are adorned with intricate carvings, showcasing the wealth and status of the merchants who lived there centuries ago.

CHALLENGE NO. 9

WATCH A MOVIE IN HINDI WITHOUT ENGLISH SUBTITLES AND SUMMARIZE THE STORY.

"हर छोटी सफलता का जश्न मनाओ, यही बड़ी सफलता की ओर ले जाता है।"

"Celebrate every small success, it leads to greater achievements."

दिन 91: शॉपिंग और दुकानें

1. **दुकान** पर चलोगे?
2. हाँ, **सुपरमार्केट** में क्या खरीदना है?
3. **शॉपिंग मॉल** में **सेल** है, **छूट** पर कपड़े देखने हैं।
4. अच्छा, **टोकरी** ले लो या **गाड़ी**?
5. **गाड़ी** बेहतर है, ज्यादा सामान होगा।
6. **कैशियर** के पास **रसीद** जरूर लेना।
7. हाँ, और **कीमत** भी चेक कर लेंगे।
8. चलो, जल्दी करो, घर भी जाना है।

✣ In Hindi, to indicate location while talking about shopping and stores, use the postposition "में" (mein) after the name of the place, as in "मैं दुकान में हूँ" (I am in the store).

1. **dukāna** para calogē?
2. hām̐, **suparmārkeṭa** mēṁ kyā kharīdanā hai?
3. **śŏpiṅga mŏla** mēṁ **sēla** hai, **chūṭa** para kapṛē dēkhanē haim̐.
4. acchā, **ṭōkarī** lē lō yā **gāṛī**?
5. **gāṛī** bēhtara hai, jyādā sāmāna hōgā.
6. **kaiśiyara** kē pāsa **rasīda** jarūra lēnā.
7. hām̐, aura **kīmata** bhī cēka kara lēṅgē.
8. calō, jaldī karō, ghara bhī jānā hai.

1. Will you go to the **store**?
2. Yes, what do we need to buy at the **supermarket**?
3. There's a **sale** in the **shopping mall**, want to check out clothes on **discount**.
4. Okay, should we take a **basket** or a **cart**?
5. A **cart** is better, we'll have more stuff.
6. Make sure to get a **receipt** from the **cashier**.
7. Yes, and we'll also check the **prices**.
8. Let's hurry, we need to go home too.

✣ In ancient India, the concept of "Hundi," an indigenous financial instrument, facilitated trade by allowing merchants to safely transfer money without physically moving currency, revolutionizing the retail and trade sectors.

दिन 92: आपातकाल और सुरक्षा

1. **आपातकाल** है! **आग** लग गई है।
2. **पुलिस** को फोन करो।
3. **एम्बुलेंस** और **डॉक्टर** की जरूरत है।
4. **सहायता** के लिए मैं क्या करूं?
5. **प्राथमिक चिकित्सा** बॉक्स कहाँ है?
6. वह अलमारी में है। **सुरक्षित** रहें।
7. **अस्पताल** ले चलें जो घायल हैं।
8. **खतरा** अभी भी है, बाहर निकलें!
9. हां, चलो यहां से निकलते हैं।

✤ In Hindi, to express purpose or reason, often "के लिए" (ke liye) is used at the end of a clause.

1. **āpātakāla** hai! **āga** laga gaī hai.
2. **pulisa** ko phona karo.
3. **embulēnsa** aura **ḍākṭara** kī jarūrata hai.
4. **sahāyatā** ke lie maiṁ kyā karūṁ?
5. **prāthamika cikitsā** bŏksa kahām̐ hai?
6. vaha alamārī meṁ hai. **surakṣita** raheṁ.
7. **aspatāla** le caleṁ jo ghāyala haiṁ.
8. **khatara** abhī bhī hai, bāhara nikaleṁ!
9. hām̐, calo yahām̐ se nikalate haiṁ.

1. **Emergency**! There's a **fire**.
2. Call the **police**.
3. We need an **ambulance** and a **doctor**.
4. What should I do to help?
5. Where is the **first aid** box?
6. It's in the cupboard. Stay **safe**.
7. Take those who are injured to the **hospital**.
8. The **danger** is still present, get out!
9. Yes, let's get out of here.

✣ In ancient Indian epics, the monkey god Hanuman is celebrated for his heroic rescue of Sita from the demon king Ravana.

1. **पासपोर्ट** और **वीजा** तैयार हैं?
2. हां, और **होटल** का **रिजर्वेशन** भी कर लिया है।
3. **टिकट** कहां हैं?
4. मेरे **बैकपैक** में हैं। **सामान** और **सूटकेस** तुम ले आओ।
5. **पर्यटक** के लिए **नक्शा** जरूरी है।
6. हां, मैंने **गाइड** बुक कर लिया है।
7. **टैक्सी** कब आएगी?
8. **अभी** पांच मिनट में।
9. चलो, **हवाई अड्डे** के लिए देर न हो जाए।

✤ In Hindi, to express a concessive clause related to travel and places, we often use "हालांकि" or "परन्तु" at the beginning of a sentence, meaning "although" or "but".

1. **pāsapōrṭa** aura **vījā** taiyāra haiṁ?
2. hām̐, aura **hoṭala** kā **rijarvēśana** bhī kara liyā hai.
3. **ṭikaṭa** kahām̐ haiṁ?
4. mērē **baikapaika** mēṁ haiṁ. **sāmāna** aura **sūṭakēsa** tuma lē ā'ō.
5. **paryaṭaka** kē li'ē **nakśā** jarūrī hai.
6. hām̐, mainnē **gā'iḍa** buka kara liyā hai.
7. **ṭaiksī** kaba ā'ēgī?
8. **abhī** pām̐ca minaṭa mēṁ.
9. calō, **havā'ī aḍḍē** kē li'ē dēra na hō jā'ē.

DAY 93: TRAVEL AND PLACES III

1. **Passport** and **visa** ready?
2. Yes, and the **hotel reservation** is also done.
3. Where are the **tickets**?
4. They are in my **backpack**. Bring the **luggage** and **suitcase**.
5. A **map** is essential for a **tourist**.
6. Yes, I have booked a **guide**.
7. When will the **taxi** arrive?
8. In **just** five minutes.
9. Let's go, so we don't get late for the **airport**.

✤ The Taj Mahal Palace in Mumbai, opened in 1903, was the first hotel in India to have electricity.

दिन 94: जानवर और पालतू जानवर

1. आज मैंने **बिल्ली** और **कुत्ते** खरीदे।
2. अच्छा! मेरे पास **पक्षी** और **मछलियाँ** हैं।
3. तुम्हारा **घोड़ा** कैसा है?
4. वह बहुत प्रसन्न है। और तुम्हारी **गाय**?
5. मेरी **गाय** भी संतुष्ट है।
6. क्या तुमने **भेड़** और **बकरियाँ** भी देखीं?
7. हाँ, मैंने देखीं। मेरी **मुर्गी** अकेली है।
8. ओह, मेरी **सुअर** भी अकेला है।
9. चलो, हम उन्हें साथ में रखते हैं।

✤ In Hindi, to add an explanatory clause about animals or pets, use "jo" (जो) to introduce the clause, as in "Mera kutta, jo bada hai, bahut bhonkta hai" (मेरा कुत्ता, जो बड़ा है, बहुत भौंकता है) meaning "My dog, who is big, barks a lot."

1. āja mainne **billī** aura **kutte** kharīde.
2. acchā! mere pāsa **pakṣī** aura **machaliyām̐** haim̐.
3. tumhārā **ghoṛā** kaisā hai?
4. vaha bahuta prasanna hai. aura tumhārī **gāya**?
5. merī **gāya** bhī santuṣṭa hai.
6. kyā tumne **bheṛa** aura **bakariyām̐** bhī dekhīm̐?
7. hām̐, mainne dekhīm̐. merī **murgī** akelī hai.
8. oha, merī **sūara** bhī akelā hai.
9. calo, hama unhem̐ sātha mem̐ rakhte haim̐.

DAY 94: ANIMALS AND PETS

1. Today, I bought a **cat** and a **dog**.
2. Oh! I have **birds** and **fish**.
3. How is your **horse**?
4. He is very happy. And your **cow**?
5. My **cow** is also content.
6. Did you see the **sheep** and **goats** too?
7. Yes, I saw them. My **chicken** is lonely.
8. Oh, my **pig** is lonely too.
9. Let's keep them together.

✤ In ancient Indian epic Mahabharata, the monkey god Hanuman is a symbol of strength and loyalty.

1. **कार्यालय** में आज **नौकरी** का पहला दिन है।
2. हाँ, **कर्मचारी** बनकर अच्छा लग रहा है।
3. **मालिक** से मिले?
4. हाँ, उन्होंने **सहकर्मी** से मिलवाया।
5. **बैठक** कब है?
6. कल, **समय सीमा** से पहले **रिपोर्ट** तैयार करनी होगी।
7. **सम्मेलन** के लिए **प्रस्तुतिकरण** भी बनाना है।
8. चिंता मत करो, साथ में करेंगे।
9. धन्यवाद, सहायता के लिए।

✤ In direct speech, we use quotation marks to enclose the exact words spoken by a person, for example, the carpenter said, "I will finish the work by tomorrow."

1. **kāryālaya** meṃ āja **naukrī** kā pahalā dina hai.
2. hāṁ, **karmacārī** banakara acchā laga rahā hai.
3. **mālika** se mile?
4. hāṁ, unhoṁne **sahakarmī** se milavāyā.
5. **baiṭhaka** kaba hai?
6. kala, **samaya sīmā** se pahale **ripōrṭa** tayāra karanī hogī.
7. **sammelana** ke lie **prasṭutikaraṇa** bhī banānā hai.
8. cintā mata karo, sātha meṃ kareṅge.
9. dhanyavāda, sahāyatā ke lie.

1. Today is the first day of **work** at the **office**.
2. Yes, it feels good to be an **employee**.
3. Met the **boss**?
4. Yes, they introduced me to a **colleague**.
5. When is the **meeting**?
6. Tomorrow, the **report** must be prepared before the **deadline**.
7. Also have to make a **presentation** for the **conference**.
8. Don't worry, we'll do it together.
9. Thank you for the help.

✤ Mahatma Gandhi, originally a lawyer, significantly altered the course of Indian history through non-violent resistance.

दिन 96: दिन और महीने

1. **सोमवार** को तुम कार्यालय जाओगे?
2. हां, मेरे सहकर्मी और मैं **जनवरी** में एक परियोजना पर काम कर रहे हैं।
3. **मंगलवार** को मालिक से मिलना है।
4. अच्छा, **बुधवार** को मेरा वीजा इंटरव्यू है।
5. तुम्हारा टिकट और सामान तैयार है?
6. हां, **गुरुवार** को सब चेक कर लूंगा।
7. **शुक्रवार** को मेरे दोस्त आ रहे हैं।
8. **शनिवार** और **रविवार** को हम त्योहार मनाएंगे।
9. बहुत अच्छा, **मार्च** में मिलते हैं।

✤ In indirect speech, when talking about days and months, we change "today" to "that day" and "this month" to "that month."

1. **somavāra** ko tuma kāryālaya jāoge?
2. hām̐, mere sahakarmī aura mãī **janavarī** meṁ eka pariyojanā para kāma kara rahe haiṁ.
3. **maṅgalavāra** ko mālika se milanā hai.
4. acchā, **budhavāra** ko merā vījā inṭaravyū hai.
5. tumhārā ṭikaṭa aura sāmāna taiyāra hai?
6. hām̐, **guruvāra** ko saba ceka kara lūm̐gā.
7. **śukravāra** ko mere dost ā rahe haiṁ.
8. **śanivāra** aura **ravivāra** ko hama tyohāra manāeṅge.
9. bahuta acchā, **mārca** meṁ milate haiṁ.

1. Will you go to the office on **Monday**?
2. Yes, my colleague and I are working on a project in **January**.
3. I have a meeting with the boss on **Tuesday**.
4. Okay, I have my visa interview on **Wednesday**.
5. Is your ticket and luggage ready?
6. Yes, I will check everything on **Thursday**.
7. My friends are coming on **Friday**.
8. We will celebrate the festival on **Saturday** and **Sunday**.
9. Great, see you in **March**.

✤ Ancient Hindu calendars were based on lunar months and solar years, intricately aligning celestial and terrestrial events.

दिन 97: शरीर और स्वास्थ्य

1. क्या तुम्हारा **सिर** दर्द कर रहा है?
2. हां, और मेरी **उंगली** भी चोटिल है।
3. तुम्हें आराम करना चाहिए। तुम्हारे **हाथ** में दर्द है क्या?
4. नहीं, लेकिन मेरी **बांह** में थोड़ा दर्द है।
5. तुम्हारी **आंख** लाल क्यों है?
6. मैंने **धूप का चश्मा** नहीं पहना था।
7. और तुम्हारी **नाक**?
8. मैंने बगीचे में **फूल** सूंघे थे।
9. अच्छा, जल्दी से ठीक हो जाओ।

✣ In Hindi, Free Indirect Speech blends the character's thoughts or speech into the narrative without using quotation marks, allowing for a seamless transition between the narrator's words and the character's inner thoughts, especially when describing feelings or conditions related to body and health.

1. kyā tumhārā **sira** dard kar rahā hai?
2. hāṁ, aura merī **uṅglī** bhī coṭil hai.
3. tumheṁ ārām karnā cāhie. tumhāre **hāth** meṁ dard hai kyā?
4. nahīṁ, lekin merī **bāṁh** meṁ thoṛā dard hai.
5. tumhārī **āṁkh** lāl kyoṁ hai?
6. maine **dhūp kā caśmā** nahīṁ pahnā thā.
7. aura tumhārī **nāk**?
8. maine bagīce meṁ **phūl** sūṅghe the.
9. achchhā, jaldī se ṭhīk ho jāo.

1. Is your **head** hurting?
2. Yes, and my **finger** is also injured.
3. You should rest. Do you have pain in your **hand**?
4. No, but my **arm** is a bit sore.
5. Why is your **eye** red?
6. I didn't wear **sunglasses**.
7. And your **nose**?
8. I was smelling **flowers** in the garden.
9. Alright, get well soon.

✤ In rural India, kabaddi, a team sport without any equipment, has been traditionally played for centuries, fostering community spirit and physical fitness.

दिन ९८: शिक्षा और सीखने का दूसरा भाग

1. आज कक्षा में हम शिक्षा के महत्व पर चर्चा करेंगे। तुम्हारी किताब कहाँ है?
2. मेरी किताब मेरे बस्ते में है। मैं अभी निकालता हूँ।
3. ठीक है, और होमवर्क किया?
4. हाँ, मैंने कलम और पेंसिल से कॉपी में होमवर्क पूरा किया।
5. बहुत अच्छा। परीक्षा के लिए तैयार हो?
6. जी हाँ, मैंने पढ़ाई की है।
7. शिक्षा से हमें ज्ञान मिलता है। तुम एक अच्छे विद्यार्थी हो।
8. धन्यवाद, सर। मैं और अधिक सीखना चाहता हूँ।

✤ In Hindi, the verb must agree with the subject in both number and gender.

1. āja kakṣā mēṁ hama śikṣā kē mahatva para carcā karēṅgē. tumhārī kitāba kahām̐ hai?
2. mērī kitāba mērē bastē mēṁ hai. maiṁ abhī nikālatā hūm̐.
3. ṭhīka hai, aura hōmavar̥ka kiyā?
4. hām̐, mainnē kalam̐ aura pēnsila sē kāpī mēṁ hōmavar̥ka pūrā kiyā.
5. bahuta acchā. parīkṣā kē liē taiyāra hō?
6. jī hām̐, mainnē paṛhā'ī kī hai.
7. śikṣā sē hamēṁ jñāna milatā hai. tuma ēka acchē vidyārthī hō.
8. dhanyavāda, sara. maiṁ aura adhika sīkhanā cāhatā hūm̐.

1. Today in class, we will discuss the importance of education. Where is your book?
2. My book is in my bag. I'll take it out now.
3. Alright, and have you done your homework?
4. Yes, I completed the homework in my notebook with a pen and pencil.
5. Very good. Are you ready for the exam?
6. Yes, I have studied.
7. Education gives us knowledge. You are a good student.
8. Thank you, sir. I want to learn more.

✣ Rabindranath Tagore, a renowned philosopher and educator, founded an innovative school in Shantiniketan, India, emphasizing creativity and holistic education.

दिन 99: विविध II

1. **उत्सव** कब है?
2. **त्योहार** शुक्रवार को है।
3. तुम **उपहार** लाओगे?
4. हां, मैं **चाबी** का गुच्छा लाऊंगा।
5. **समारोह** में **संगीत** होगा?
6. जी हां, और **नृत्य** भी होगा।
7. **छुट्टी** मिलेगी?
8. हां, स्कूल बंद रहेगा।
9. **परंपरा** के अनुसार, सब **ताले** खोलेंगे।

✤ In Hindi, the typical sentence structure follows the Subject-Object-Verb (SOV) order.

1. **utsava** kab hai?
2. **tyōhāra** śukravāra kō hai.
3. tum **upahāra** lā'ōgē?
4. hāṁ, maiṁ **cābī** kā gucchā lā'ūṅgā.
5. **samārōha** mēṁ **saṅgīta** hōgā?
6. jī hāṁ, aura **nr̥tya** bhī hōgā.
7. **chuṭṭī** milēgī?
8. hāṁ, skūla band rahēgā.
9. **paraṁparā** kē anusāra, saba **tālē** khōlēṅgē.

1. When is the **festival**?
2. The **festival** is on Friday.
3. Will you bring a **gift**?
4. Yes, I will bring a bunch of **keys**.
5. Will there be **music** at the **ceremony**?
6. Yes, there will be **dance** as well.
7. Will we get a **holiday**?
8. Yes, the school will be closed.
9. According to **tradition**, everyone will unlock the **locks**.

✤ In ancient India, chess was invented as a game called "Chaturanga," symbolizing the four divisions of the military.

दिन 100: मैनुअल पूरा करने के लिए बधाई हो

1. मैनुअल पूरा करने के लिए बधाई हो।
2. धन्यवाद! क्या तुमने **किताब** पढ़ी?
3. हां, मैंने **कंप्यूटर** पर पढ़ी।
4. **कॉफी** पियोगे?
5. हां, और क्या तुम **पानी** पियोगे?
6. नहीं, मैं भी **कॉफी** पियूंगा। **कार** की चाबी देखी?
7. नहीं, शायद **कुर्सी** के पास होगी।
8. अच्छा, मैं **खिड़की** खोल देता हूँ, ताज़ा हवा आएगी।
9. बहुत अच्छा, फिर हम **संगीत** भी सुनेंगे।

✤ In Hindi, verbs change form to match the subject in both number and gender.

1. mainual pūrā karṇe ke liye badhāī ho.
2. dhanyavād! kyā tumne **kitāb** paṛhī?
3. hāṁ, maiṇe **kaṁpyūṭar** par paṛhī.
4. **kāphī** piyoge?
5. hāṁ, aur kyā tum **pānī** piyoge?
6. nahīṁ, maiṁ bhī **kāphī** pīūṁgā. **kār** kī cābī dekhī?
7. nahīṁ, śāyad **kursī** ke pās hogī.
8. achchhā, maiṁ **khiṛkī** khol detā hūṁ, tāzā havā āyegī.
9. bahut achchhā, phir ham **saṁgīt** bhī sunenge.

DAY 100: CONGRATULATIONS ON COMPLETING THE MANUAL

1. Congratulations on completing the manual.
2. Thank you! Did you read the **book**?
3. Yes, I read it on the **computer**.
4. Will you have some **coffee**?
5. Yes, and will you have some **water**?
6. No, I'll also have **coffee**. Seen the **car** keys?
7. No, maybe they are near the **chair**.
8. Alright, I'll open the **window** to let in some fresh air.
9. Very good, then we'll also listen to some **music**.

✣ In Hindi culture, achieving success is often celebrated with the sweet distribution of "laddoos," symbolizing the sharing of joy.

CHALLENGE NO. 10

PREPARE AND GIVE AN ORAL PRESENTATION IN HINDI ON A TOPIC YOU ARE PASSIONATE ABOUT AND RECORD YOURSELF.

"नई संस्कृतियों का अन्वेषण करना, आत्मा को विस्तार देता है।"

"Exploring new cultures expands the soul."

CONGRATULATIONS AND NEXT STEPS

CONGRATULATIONS

Congratulations on completing the 100 days of learning Hindi! Your determination and perseverance have led you to succeed in this linguistic adventure.

You are now immersed in Hindi and have acquired a solid vocabulary base, enabling you to understand and communicate in most everyday situations. This is a remarkable achievement in such a short time!

Throughout the lessons, you have developed mental mechanisms that encourage spontaneous understanding and natural conversation in Hindi.

Be proud of yourself. You have achieved a level of autonomy that fully opens up the doors to the language and culture of Hindi.

The adventure continues! To maintain and refine your skills in Hindi:

- Practice translating texts from English to Hindi.

- Listen to our audios on shuffle to strengthen and refresh your vocabulary.
- Immerse yourself in the language: watch Bollywood movies and listen to podcasts in Hindi.
- If you're using Flashcards, continue their daily use.
- Communicate in Hindi, with native speakers or via AI.

Congratulations again on this achievement! And see you soon in your continuous learning journey. Namaste.

WHAT'S NEXT?

Your success is undeniable, and to maintain your skills, continuous practice is essential.

Here are some ideas to continue progressing:

1. Review the vocabulary from this manual with our Flashcards.
2. Elevate your skills to a new level by discovering our intermediate-level manual or by exploring other NaturaLingua resources.
3. Join our online community: share, learn, and inspire others. Your journey can enlighten new learners.
4. Watch our video training and discover the secrets to mastering a language in just 100 days.
5. Fully immerse yourself in the language to reach new heights.

6. If you're ready for a new challenge, why not start a new language with our "Learn a Language in 100 Days" collection?

Learning a language is an endless adventure. Whether you deepen your knowledge of this language or embark on a new linguistic journey, the voyage never ends.

Congratulations and good luck on your continued journey!

ADDITIONAL RESOURCES

DOWNLOAD THE RESOURCES ASSOCIATED WITH THIS MANUAL AND GREATLY ENHANCE YOUR CHANCES OF SUCCESS.

Scan this QR code to access them:

SCAN ME

https://www.natura-lingua.com/download

- **Optimize your learning with audio:** To significantly improve your language skills, we strongly advise you to download the audio files accompanying this manual. This will enhance your listening comprehension and pronunciation.

• **Enhance your learning with flashcards:** Flashcards are excellent tools for vocabulary memorization. We highly encourage you to use them to maximize your results. Download our set of cards, specially designed for this manual.

• **Join our learning community:** If you're looking to connect with other language enthusiasts through "Natura Lingua", we invite you to join our online group. In this community, you'll have the opportunity to ask questions, find learning partners, and share your progress.

• **Explore more with other Natura Lingua manuals:** If you like this method, note that there are other similar manuals for different languages. Discover our complete collection of manuals to enrich your linguistic learning experience in a natural and progressive way.

We are here to support you in learning the target language. For optimal results, we highly recommend downloading the audio and using the flashcards. These additional resources are designed to further facilitate your journey.

Happy learning!

ABOUT THE AUTHOR

François Trésorier is a passionate polyglot and an expert in accelerated learning. He has developed unique learning methods that have helped over 31,400 people in more than 94 countries quickly achieve their learning objectives.

With more than 7 years of research, testing, and developing innovative approaches for rapid language learning, he created the Natura Lingua method. This intuitive and natural method, based on the latest findings in cognition, enables quick language results.

When he's not creating new language learning manuals or helping his community achieve language results, François is involved in humanitarian efforts in the south and east of Ukraine.

Discover how the Natura Lingua method can transform your language learning.

Visit our website www.natura-lingua.com and join our dynamic community of passionate learners.

SHARE YOUR EXPERIENCE

Help Us Revolutionize Language Learning

I hope you found this manual enriching and useful. Our goal is to democratize this innovative and natural approach to language learning, to help as many people as possible quickly and easily achieve their linguistic goals. Your support is crucial for us. If you enjoyed this manual, we would be deeply grateful if you could take a moment to leave a review on Amazon KDP. Your feedback is not only a source of encouragement for us but also helps other language learners discover this method. Thank you immensely for your contribution to our project and best wishes on your language learning journey!

BY THE SAME AUTHOR

FIND ALL OUR NATURALINGUA BOOKS ON OUR WEBSITE

SCAN ME

We regularly add new titles to our collection. Feel free to visit our website to discover the latest releases:

http://www.natura-lingua.com/

This list is not exhaustive:

- English in 100 Days
- Spanish in 100 Days
- German in 100 Days
- Italian in 100 Days
- Portuguese in 100 Days
- Dutch in 100 Days
- Arabic in 100 Days
- Russian in 100 Days
- Chinese in 100 Days
- Japanese in 100 Days
- Korean in 100 Days

- Ukrainian in 100 Days
- Turkish in 100 Days
- Swedish in 100 Days
- Norwegian in 100 Days
- Danish in 100 Days
- Polish in 100 Days
- Hebrew in 100 Days
- Greek in 100 Days
- Romanian in 100 Days
- Vietnamese in 100 Days

ESSENTIAL GLOSSARY

INDISPENSABLE WORDS AND THEIR MEANINGS

Above - ऊपर
Actor/Actress - अभिनेता/अभिनेत्री
Afternoon - दोपहर
Airplane - हवाई जहाज
Airport - हवाई अड्डा
Allergy - एलर्जी
Alone - अकेला/अकेली
Alone - अकेला
Ambulance - एम्बुलेंस
And - और
And you? - और आप?
Angry - गुस्सा
Angry - क्रोधित
Animal - पशु
Anxious - चिंतित
Apartment - अपार्टमेंट
App - एप्लिकेशन
Appetizer - सोफ़ा
Appetizer - स्टार्टर
Application - एप्लिकेशन
April - अप्रैल
Arm - बाजू
Arm - बांह
Arrival - आगमन
Assistant - सहायता
ATM - एटीएम
August - अगस्त
Aunt - चाची या मौसी या बुआ या मामी
Aunt - चाची/मौसी/बुआ/ताई
Author - लेखक/लेखिका
Autumn - पतझड़
Back - पीठ
Backpack - बैकपैक
Backpack - बस्ता
Bad - बुरा
Baked - बेक्ड
Balcony - बालकनी
Band - बैंड
Bank - बैंक
Banknote - नोट
Bar - बार
Basket - टोकरी
Bathroom - बाथरूम
Beach - समुद्र तट
Bed - बिस्तर
Beef - गाय का मांस
Beer - बीयर
Behind - पीछे
Beside - बगल में
Between - के बीच
Bicycle - साइकिल
Big - बड़ा
Bike - साइकिल
Bird - पक्षी

Black - काला
Blog - ब्लॉग
Blue - नीला
Boarding pass - बोर्डिंग पास
Boat - नाव
Book - किताब
Boss - मालिक
Brain - दिमाग
Bread - रोटी
Brother - भाई
Brown - भूरा
Browser - ब्राउज़र
Bus - बस
Butter - मक्खन
Buy - खरीदना
Cake - केक
Calendar - कैलेंडर
Calendar - पंचांग
Calm - शांत
Camera - कैमरा
Canyon - घाटी
Car - कार
Cart - गाड़ी
Cash - नकद
Cashier - कैशियर
Casual - आरामदायक
Cat - बिल्ली
Cave - गुफा
Ceiling - छत
Celebration - समारोह
Centimeter - सेंटीमीटर
Chair - कुर्सी
Channel - चैनल
Cheap - सस्ता
Checkout - कैश काउंटर
Cheese - पनीर
Chef - शेफ
Chest - छाती
Chicken - चिकन
Chicken - मुर्गी
Children - बच्चे
Chocolate - चॉकलेट
Chocolate : Chocolate - Chocolate : चॉकलेट
Cinema - सिनेमा
Classroom - कक्षा
Climate - मौसम
Climate - जलवायु
Clinic - क्लिनिक
Clock - घड़ी
Close - पास
Clothes - कपड़े
Cloud - बादल
Coffee - कॉफ़ी
Coffee - कॉफी

Coin - सिक्का	Cold - ठंडा	Colleague - सहकर्मी
Computer - कंप्यूटर	Concert - कॉन्सर्ट	Conference - सम्मेलन
Confused - भ्रमित	Content - संतुष्ट	Continent - महाद्वीप
Cough - खांसी	Courtyard - आँगन	Cousin - चचेरा भाई या चचेरी बहन
Cousin - चचेरा भाई/चचेरी बहन/ममेरा भाई/ममेरी बहन/फुफेरा भाई/फुफेरी बहन	Cousin - चचेरा भाई/चचेरी बहन	Cow - गाय
Credit card - क्रेडिट कार्ड	Culture - संस्कृति	Currency - मुद्रा
Dance - नृत्य	Danger - खतरा	Day - दिन
Deadline - समय सीमा	Debit card - डेबिट कार्ड	December - दिसंबर
Delayed - विलंबित	Delighted - प्रसन्न	Dentist - दंत चिकित्सक
Departure - प्रस्थान	Desert - रेगिस्तान	Dessert - मिठाई
Discount - छूट	Doctor - डॉक्टर	Doctor - डॉक्टर
Dog - कुत्ता	Door - दरवाज़ा	Down - नीचे
Download - डाउनलोड करना	Download - डाउनलोड	Drawing - चित्र
Drink - पेय	Drink - पीना	Drizzle - बूंदाबांदी
Dry - सूखा	Ear - कान	Earrings - झुमके
Earrings - बालियाँ	Earthquake - भूकंप	Egg - अंडा
Eight - आठ	Eighteen - अठारह	Eleven - ग्यारह
Email - ईमेल	Embassy - दूतावास	Emergency - आपातकाल

Employee - कर्मचारी	Evening - शाम	Exam - परीक्षा
Exchange rate - विनिमय दर	Excited - उत्साहित	Excuse me - क्षमा कीजिये
Expensive - महंगा	Eye - आँख	Eye - आंख
Face - चेहरा	Family - परिवार	Far - दूर
Fast - तेज	Fast - तेज़	Father - पिता
February - फरवरी	Festival - त्योहार	Fever - बुखार
Fiancé/Fiancée - मंगेतर	Fiction - काल्पनिक	Fifteen - पंद्रह
Finger - उंगली	Fire - आग	Fire - आग
First aid - प्राथमिक चिकित्सा	Fish - मछली	Fitting room - ट्रायल रूम
Five - पांच	Floor - फर्श	Flower - फूल
Foot - पैर	Foot - पैर का पंजा	Forecast - पूर्वानुमान
Forecast - मौसम का पूर्वानुमान	Forest - जंगल	Forest - वन
Fork - कांटा	Forty - चालीस	Four - चार
Fourteen - चौदह	Freezer - फ्रीजर	Friday - शुक्रवार
Fried - तला हुआ	Friend - दोस्त	Friends - दोस्त
Fruit - फल	Fruits - फल	Full - भरा हुआ
Garage - गैराज	Garden - बगीचा	Gate - द्वार
Gift - उपहार	Goat - बकरी	Gold - सोना

Good - अच्छा

Good afternoon - नमस्ते

Good evening - शुभ संध्या

Good night - शुभ रात्रि

Goodbye - अलविदा

Granddaughter - पोती

Grandparents - दादा-दादी

Grandson - पोता

Grass - घास

Green - हरा

Grey - धूसर

Grilled - ग्रिल्ड

Grocery store - किराना दुकान

Grocery store - किराना की दुकान

Guide - गाइड

Hair - बाल

Hand - हाथ

Happy - खुश

Happy - प्रसन्न

Hard - कठिन

Hat - टोपी

Have a good day - आपका दिन शुभ हो

Head - सिर

Headache - सिरदर्द

Heavy - भारी

Height - ऊंचाई

Hello - नमस्ते

Here - यहाँ

Hi - नमस्ते

Hiking - ट्रेकिंग

History - इतिहास

Holiday - छुट्टी

Homework - होमवर्क

Horse - घोड़ा

Hospital - अस्पताल

Hospital - अस्पताल

Hot - गर्म

Hotel - होटल

Hour - घंटा

House - घर

How are you? - आप कैसे हैं?

How much does it cost? - यह कितने का है?

How much? - कितना?

How old are you? - आपकी उम्र क्या है?

How? - कैसे?

Humid - नम

Hurricane - चक्रवात

Husband - पति

I am - मैं हूँ

I am [age] years old - मेरी उम्र [उम्र] साल है

I am a [profession] - मैं [व्यवसाय] हूँ

I am fine - मैं ठीक हूँ

I am from [city/country] - मैं [शहर/देश] से हूँ

I am going - जा रहा हूँ

I buy - मैं खरीदता हूँ

I can - मैं कर सकता हूँ

I give - मैं देता हूँ

I have - मेरे पास है

I know - मुझे पता है

I like music and sports - मुझे संगीत और खेल पसंद हैं

I live in [city/country] - मैं [शहर/देश] मैं रहता हूँ

I love you - मैं तुमसे प्यार करता हूँ

I miss you - मुझे तुम्हारी याद आती है

I need - मुझे ज़रूरत है

I understand - समझता हूँ

I watch - मैं देख रहा हूँ

I would like - मैं चाहूँगा

I'm joking - मैं मजाक कर रहा हूँ

Ice cream - आइसक्रीम

Ice-cream : Ice Cream - Ice-cream : आइसक्रीम

In - अंदर

Inch - इंच

Indigenous - आदिवासी

Injury - चोट

Inn - सराय

Inside - अंदर

Internet - इंटरनेट

Island - द्वीप

Jacket - जैकेट

Jam - जैम

January - जनवरी

Jewelry - आभूषण

Job - नौकरी

Joyful - प्रसन्न

Juice - रस

Juice : Juice - Juice : रस

July - जुलाई

June - जून

Jungle - जंगल

Key - चाबी

Kilogram - किलोग्राम

Kitchen - रसोई

Knee - घुटना

Knife - चाकू

Lake - झील

Lamp - लैंप

Laptop - लैपटॉप

Large - बड़ा

Lawyer - वकील

Leaf - पत्ता

Left - बाएँ

Leg - पैर

Leg - टांग

Length - लंबाई

Lesson - पाठ

Light - हल्का

Lightning - बिजली

Liquid - तरल

Living room - लिविंग रूम

Lock - ताला

Long - लंबा

Look - देखना

Loud - शोरीला

Low - नीचा

Luggage - सामान

Main course - मुख्य व्यंजन

Man - आदमी

Manager - प्रबंधक/प्रबंधिका

Map - नक्शा

March - मार्च

Market - बाजार

May - मई

Maybe - शायद

Meat - मांस

Medicine - दवा

Meeting - बैठक

Menu - मेन्यू

Meter - मीटर

Midnight - आधी रात

Milk - दूध

Milk : Milk - Milk : दूध

Minute - मिनट

Monday - सोमवार

Month - महीना

Morning - सुबह

Mother - माँ

Mountain - पहाड़

Mouse - चूहा

Mouth - मुँह

Mouth - मुंह

Movie - फिल्म

Museum - संग्रहालय

Music - संगीत

My name is... - मेरा नाम... है

Near - नज़दीक

Neck - गर्दन

Necklace - हार

Neighbor - पड़ोसी

Nephew - भतीजा

Nervous - घबराया हुआ/घबरायी हुई

Nervous - घबराया हुआ

New - नया

News - समाचार

Nice to meet you! - मिलकर अच्छा लगा!

Niece - भतीजी

Night - रात

Nine - नौ

Nineteen - उन्नीस

No - नहीं

Non-fiction - गैर-काल्पनिक

Noon - दोपहर

Nose - नाक

Notebook - कॉपी
Novel - उपन्यास
November - नवंबर
Now - अभी
Ocean - महासागर
October - अक्टूबर
Office - कार्यालय
Okay - ठीक है
Old - पुराना
On the left - बाएँ
On the right - दाएँ
One - एक
Online - ऑनलाइन
Orange - नारंगी
Oven - ओवन
Over there - वहाँ
Painting - चित्रकला
Pan - तवा
Parents - माता-पिता
Park - पार्क
Partner - साझेदार
Partner - साथी
Party - उत्सव
Passport - पासपोर्ट
Password - पासवर्ड
Pasta - पास्ता
Pastry : Pastry - Pastry : पेस्ट्री
Pen - कलम
Pencil - पेंसिल
Pepper - काली मिर्च
Pharmacy - फार्मेसी
Photography - फोटोग्राफी
Pie : Pie - Pie : पाई
Pig - सूअर
Pig - सुअर
Pill - गोली
Pink - गुलाबी
Plane - हवाई जहाज
Plant - पौधा
Plate - प्लेट
Plate - थाली
Play - बजाना
Play - नाटक
Play - खेलना
Please - कृपया
Poetry - कविता
Police - पुलिस
Police - पुलिस
Pond - तालाब
Pork - सूअर का मांस
Port - बंदरगाह
Prescription - पर्चा
Presentation - प्रस्तुतिकरण
President - अध्यक्ष/अध्यक्षा

Price - मूल्य
Price - कीमत
Printer - प्रिंटर
Proud - गर्वित
Radio - रेडियो
Railway station - रेलवे स्टेशन
Rain - बारिश
Rainbow - इंद्रधनुष
Reading - पाठ
Receipt - रसीद
Red - लाल
Refrigerator - फ्रिज
Refrigerator - फ़्रिज
Refund - रिफंड
Refund - वापसी
Relative - रिश्तेदार
Relaxed - आराम से
Relaxed - आराम
Remote control - रिमोट कंट्रोल
Report - रिपोर्ट
Reservation - रिजर्वेशन
Restaurant - रेस्टोरेंट
Rice - चावल
Right - दाएँ
River - नदी
Roasted - भुना हुआ
Roof - छत
Room - कमरा
Round - गोल
Sad - उदास
Safe - सुरक्षित
Salad - सलाद
Sale - सेल
Sandwich - सैंडविच
Saturday - शनिवार
Saucepan - पतीला
Scared - डरा हुआ
Schedule - समय सारिणी
Schedule - टाइमटेबल
School - स्कूल
Screen - स्क्रीन
Sea - समुद्र
Second - सेकंड
See you later - फिर मिलेंगे
Sell - बेचना
September - सितंबर
Seven - सात
Seventeen - सत्रह
Shape - शेप
Sheep - भेड़
Ship - जहाज
Shirt - शर्ट
Shoes - जूते
Shopping centre - मॉल

Shopping mall - मॉल	Shopping mall - शॉपिंग मॉल	Shoulder - कंधा
Singer - गायक/गायिका	Singing - गायन	Sister - बहन
Six - छह	Sixteen - सोलह	Size - आकार
Skiing - स्कीइंग	Skin - त्वचा	Skirt - स्कर्ट
Slow - धीमा	Small - छोटा	Smartphone - स्मार्टफोन
Snowboarding - स्नोबोर्डिंग	Snowflake - हिमकण	Social media - सोशल मीडिया
Soda - सोडा	Soda : Soft Drink - Soda : सोडा	Soft - मुलायम
Song - गाना	Song - गीत	Sorry - माफ़ कीजिये
Soup - सूप	South - ऊपर	Spoon - चम्मच
Spring - वसंत	Square - वर्गाकार	Stairs - सीढ़ी
Station - रेलवे स्टेशन	Stop - रुकें	Stop here - यहाँ रुकें
Store - दुकान	Storm - आंधी	Storm - तूफान
Straight ahead - सीधे	Stream - नाला	Stressed - तनावग्रस्त
Student - छात्र	Student - छात्र/विद्यार्थी	Subject - विषय
Subway - मेट्रो	Suitcase - सूटकेस	Summer - गर्मी
Sunday - रविवार	Sunglasses - धूप का चश्मा	Sunshine - धूप
Supermarket - सुपरमार्केट	Swimming - तैराकी	Table - मेज़
Tall - ऊँचा	Taxi - टैक्सी	Tea - चाय

Teacher - अध्यापक/अध्यापिका

Teacher - अध्यापक

Teacher - अध्यापक/शिक्षक

Telephone - फोन

Television - टेलीविजन

Television - टेलीविज़न

Ten - दस

Terminal - टर्मिनल

Thank you - धन्यवाद

thank you! - धन्यवाद!

That way - उधर

The day after tomorrow - परसों

Theater - रंगमंच

There - वहाँ

Thirteen - तेरह

Thirty - तीस

Thirty-Eight - अड़तीस

Thirty-Five - पैंतीस

Thirty-Four - चौंतीस

Thirty-Nine - उनतालीस

Thirty-One - इकतीस

Thirty-Seven - सैंतीस

Thirty-Six - छत्तीस

Thirty-Three - तैंतीस

Thirty-Two - बत्तीस

This way - इधर

Three - तीन

Thrilled - प्रसन्न

Thunder - गरज

Thursday - गुरुवार

Ticket - टिकट

Time - समय

Toast - टोस्ट

Toast : Toast - Toast : टोस्ट

Toaster - टोस्टर

Today - आज

Tomorrow - कल

Tooth - दांत

Toothache - दांत दर्द

Tornado - बवंडर

Tourist - पर्यटक

Tradition - परंपरा

Train - ट्रेन

Train - रेलगाड़ी

Tram - ट्राम

Tree - पेड़

Trolley - गाड़ी

Trousers - पैंट

Truck - ट्रक

Tuesday - मंगलवार

Tuesday, - मंगलवार,

Turn - मुड़ें

Turn left - बाएँ मुड़ें

Turn right - दाएँ मुड़ें

Twelve - बारह

Twenty - बीस

Twenty-Eight - अट्ठाईस

Twenty-Five - पच्चीस

Twenty-Four - चौबीस

Twenty-Nine - उनतीस

Twenty-One - इक्कीस

Twenty-Seven - सत्ताईस

Twenty-Six - छब्बीस

Twenty-Three - तेईस

Twenty-Two - बाईस

Two - दो

Uncle - चाचा या मौसा या फूफा या मामा

Uncle - चाचा/मामा/फूफा/ताऊ

Under - नीचे

University - विश्वविद्यालय

Up - ऊपर

Upset - नाराज

Upset - परेशान

Username - उपयोगकर्ता नाम

Valley - घाटी

Vegetables - सब्ज़ियां

Vegetables - सब्जियां

Visa - वीजा

Volcano - ज्वालामुखी

Waiter/Waitress - वेटर/वेट्रेस

Wall - दीवार

Warm - गर्म

Water - पानी

Water : Water - Water : पानी

Website - वेबसाइट

Wednesday - बुधवार

Week - सप्ताह

Weekend - सप्ताहांत

Weight - वज़न

Wet - गीला

What day is it today? - आज कौन सा दिन है?

What do you do for a living? - तुम क्या करते हो?

What do you like? - तुम्हें क्या पसंद है?

What is your name? - आपका नाम क्या है?

What time is it? - क्या समय हुआ है?

What? - क्या?

When? - कब?

Where are you from? - तुम कहाँ से हो?

Where do you live? - तुम कहाँ रहते हो?

Where? - कहाँ?

Which one? - कौन सा? / कौन सी?

White - सफेद

Who? - कौन?

Why? - क्यों?

Wi-Fi - वाई-फाई

Wide - चौड़ा

Width - चौड़ाई

Wife - पत्नी